E A S T E R

INTERPRETING THE LESSONS OF THE CHURCH YEAR

DAVID BUTTRICK

PROCLAMATION 5
SERIES A

FORTRESS PRESS   MINNEAPOLIS

PROCLAMATION 5
Interpreting the Lessons of the Church Year
Series A, Easter

Cover and interior design: Spangler Design Team

Library of Congress Cataloging-in-Publication Data
(Revised for vol. [5] thru [8])

Proclamation 5.

    Contents: ser. A. [1] Epiphany / Pheme Perkins —
[2] Holy week / Robert H. Smith — [etc.] — [8] Easter /
David Buttrick.
    1. Bible—Homiletical use.   2. Bible—Liturgical
lessons, English.
BS543.5.P765   1993   251   92-22973
ISBN 0-8006-4177-9 (ser. A, Advent/Christmas)
ISBN 0-8006-4178-7 (ser. A, Epiphany)
ISBN 0-8006-4179-5 (ser. A, Lent)
ISBN 0-8006-4180-9 (ser. A, Holy week)
ISBN 0-8006-4181-7 (ser. A, Easter)
ISBN 0-8006-4182-5 (ser. A, Pentecost 1)
ISBN 0-8006-4183-3 (ser. A, Pentecost 2)
ISBN 0-8006-4184-1 (ser. A, Pentecost 3)

Manufactured in the U.S.A.   AF 1-4181

97   96   95   94   93   1   2   3   4   5   6   7   8   9   10

CONTENTS

The Resurrection of Our Lord
Easter Day

Lutheran	Roman Catholic	Episcopal	Common Lectionary
Acts 10:34-43	Acts 10:34a, 37-43	Acts 10:34-43	Acts 10:34-43 or Jer. 31:1-6
Col. 3:1-4	Col. 3:1-4	Col. 3:1-4	Col. 3:1-4 or Acts 10:34-43
John 20:1-9 or Matt. 28:1-10	John 20:1-9	John 20:1-10 or Matt. 28:1-10	John 20:1-18 or Matt. 28:1-10

FIRST LESSON: ACTS 10:34-43

Ever since Christianity happened, the question of who's in and who's out has been chronic. Every congregation, though under the evangelical mandate of the gospel, resists opening doors to those who are "not our kind of people." A we-they mentality is always a problem. Can you imagine the tensions when we-they were Jews and Gentiles? Early Christian congregations struggled over the issue and finally, with some reluctance, opened doors to welcome Gentiles. For Peter, a bit of a redneck believer, the issue was personal and intense.

God works in mysterious ways, we say. In Acts 10, God works through a brace of dreams. In one dream Cornelius is told to send messengers to Joppa asking Peter to come over to Cornelius's house for a brief speaking engagement. In the other dream Peter seems to see a bed sheet full of creatures lowered from the sky—animals and birds and, yes, even reptiles. Peter is aghast: "I have never eaten anything that is profane or unclean," he says, somewhat sanctimoniously. But a voice in the dream counters Peter's stuffiness: "What God has made clean, you must not call profane." Well, never underestimate the power of a dream. When the messengers arrive from Cornelius, Peter returns with them to give an impromptu talk. "We're all here," says Cornelius. "Let's hear what the Lord has told you to say."

Some years ago, Martin Debelius argued that all of the so-called sermons in Acts follow much the same outline: They begin with mention of the immediate situation or issue (vv. 34-35); they announce the *kerygma*, the gospel message (vv. 36-42); they allude to Scripture (v.

43a); and they usually conclude with a call to repentance (vv. 42-43b). While the outline may seem familiar, Peter's "sermon" in Cornelius's front room is quite distinctive.

In vv. 34-35 Peter refers to the issue of a Gentile mission. "God shows no partiality," he exclaims, probably citing Deut. 10:17. He goes on to remark that anyone who "does right" and fears God is acceptable. Please note: There is no mention of Christian affiliation in v. 35.

The section in vv. 36-42 seems to recapitulate Luke's story of Jesus from his birth to the commissioning of disciples after his resurrection. The verses summarize the basic content of the Christian gospel.

Verse 36, a most difficult verse to translate, declares Christ's Lordship: "he is Lord of *all.*" Some scholars suppose that v. 36 relates to the angel's announcement of Christ's birth in Luke 2; the angels spoke to shepherds—"people of Israel"—and promised "peace by Jesus Christ." In vv. 37-38, there is a summary of Jesus' ministry after his baptism: "he went about doing good and healing all who were oppressed." Notice that Peter mentions the disciples as witnesses twice. They were with Christ during his ministry, and later they were chosen witnesses to the resurrection; they "ate and drank with him after he rose from the dead," an allusion to Luke 24:30 or, more likely, Luke 24:41-43.

Acts 10:42-43 relates directly to the final chapter of Luke. In Luke the risen Christ commands the disciples to preach (24:47-48), so that all who believe may receive forgiveness (24:47). The phrase "All the prophets testify about him" also picks up Luke 24:44-45.

Of course, the big problem is, How to preach a sermon on a sermon? The argument in Peter's sermon is clear enough: (1) God is impartial, and therefore the message of salvation is to be declared to every nation and race. (2) A summary of Jesus' story demonstrates his own broad concern for the oppressed who seek righteousness and need healing. (3) The crucified, risen Lord has commanded that we preach to all, so that everyone who believes may receive mercy.

Although the outline of Peter's sermon is clear, the message today will not catch fire until it is aimed directly at our congregation's own version of exclusivism, our special forms of we-they thinking. Most oldline Protestant congregations in America are decidedly middle-class. Do we bar the doors to the poor, the barstool warmers, the raucous, to those Peter would have labeled "profane"? Are our churches racially, or patriotically, or even sexually defined—heterosexuals only, please?

No, Peter's words ring out today: God is impartial, Christ is Lord of all, so we are commanded to preach forgiveness to everyone.

SECOND LESSON: COLOSSIANS 3:1-4

What on earth has gotten into the Christians in Colossae? Have they bought into some kind of self-fulfillment cult? Perhaps. People in Colossae seem convinced that they can be filled with the fullness of God—with power and insight and virtue—if only they accept some proper spiritual disciplines, including forms of self-abasement, abstinence from particular food and drink, "days of obligation," and prayer exercises. As a result their lives are hedged by dozens of dos and don'ts—don't handle, don't taste, don't touch. "Self-imposed piety," says Paul with a snarl. The Christians in Colossae are into spirituality in the worst sense of the word, a spirituality spelled pretentiously with extra r's—spirrrrrrituality. They look up piously to angelic beings above and down scornfully at dubious earthy things like bread and wine and ethics.

So Paul (or, more likely, whoever wrote Colossians) grabs the same above-below spacial imagery and tells the Colossians to seek "things that are above." They thrill to his words. But then he adds, "where Christ is seated at the right hand of God." Oops! The creedal formula "seated at the right hand of God," drawn from Psalm 110, introduces the theme of ethical obedience. Christ, who is above, has been appointed Lord; he has authority to command our Christian lives. So to "seek those things that are above" is to take orders from the risen Christ, not angelic beings or earthly spiritual gurus.

Notice the profound logic of the passage. The Colossians are trying to save themselves via a program of "self-imposed piety, humility, and severe treatment of the body" (2:23). But Paul begins by acknowledging their salvation: "you have been raised with Christ" (3:1a). For Christians a life of obedience to Christ does not earn salvation; rather it is a way of giving thanks for salvation. Christians know that in Christ they have already died to sin and now may live toward righteousness.

Verses 3-4 are difficult. The phrase "you have died" seems to echo earlier assertions: "you were buried with him in baptism" and "you were dead in trespasses" (2:12-13). Clearly Colossians sets up a death-resurrection parallel: Just as Christ was condemned to death, buried, and yet raised up by the power of God, so we, joined to Christ, have died to sin, been buried in baptism, and now by faith are risen to live new lives. Of course, our lives are not yet fully transformed—"your life is hidden with Christ in God" (3:3b). Someday the full saving work of Christ will be revealed; then, in glory, our transformed selves will also be on display (3:4).

The notion that our lives are "hidden with Christ in God" may be difficult for a modern American congregation to grasp. Like the Colossians, we are into self-fulfillment these days. But what kind of self are we to be? Yes, as human beings we are always a work in progress. The trouble is (1) we are not ultimately in charge of the progress, and (2) we cannot envision the finished product; we have no clear idea of who we will be. Because we live in a mix of freedom and destiny, choosing and yet being chosen, God alone knows what our redeemed, risen lives will be. Ergo: Our lives are "hidden with Christ in God."

The passage in Col. 3:1-4 has been often mispreached. The contrast drawn between "above" and "on earth" (v. 2) is not a higher heavenly life versus a lower material life, the spiritual over the physical. The Bible never denigrates material things. After all, God created all things earthly and pronounced them "very good" (Gen. 1:31). No, we are creatures and need not turn away in false piety from the good physical stuff God has given us. In Col. 3:1-4 the issue is one of command: Will the risen Christ direct our lives, or will we be driven by earthly philosophies that seem so "spiritual"?

There is another theme in the passage. Paul counters the Colossian cult of self-fulfillment. Although we have been raised from self-destructive sinfulness by the power of God, we are not yet fully transformed. While we live, we are always incomplete; our true life is hidden. Yes, in a way we are already fulfilled, because our "fullness" is promised in God's saving purposes and therefore is certain. But it is emphatically not yet fulfilled, because we cannot be truly realized apart from a transformed humanity. Above all, self-fulfillment is not our project, the goal of our religious striving; it is a gift of God.

So we must no longer be captive to the world's ways of thinking, particularly the world's religious ways of thinking! We have been baptized into the new humanity, a people who take their ethical cues from Jesus Christ the risen Lord. We are to set our minds on "things above."

GOSPEL: MATTHEW 28:1-10

Most scholars insist that Matthew had a copy of Mark 16:1-8, the story of women at the tomb. But Mark's account of the resurrection ends not only in an incomplete sentence, "they were afraid for . . .," but in some theological ambiguity as well. Yes, Christ may be risen, but hold back the cheers, for disciples will still face terror and suffering before the parousia.

Matthew rewrites Mark's story. He simplifies, removes ambiguity, and at the same time heightens dramatic effect. Matthew drops one of the women, Salome, from the story, omits mention of spices to anoint the body, and skips the somewhat silly question, "Who will roll away the stone?" Instead, Matthew adds excitement—first, an earthquake and then an apocalyptic angel whose visage is "like lightning" and whose robe is "white as snow." No wonder the soldiers guarding the tomb faint. As for the women, they run away not in silence (Mark 16:8) but with "great joy," eager to tell the good news to the other disciples. To cap it all, Matthew adds an actual appearance by the risen Lord. If Mark's story is a low-budget film full of intensity, Matthew offers us a 3-D spectacular.

What about historical veracity? Did women actually show up at the tomb on Easter Day? Although the several appearance stories will not harmonize into any kind of consistent history, there is some reason to credit the women-at-the-tomb tradition. In the sexist first-century world, women were regarded as fuzzy-headed. If you wanted to validate a resurrection you certainly wouldn't pick women as witnesses. Yet, according to Scripture, women were the first to encounter the risen Christ. Thus some basis for the tradition is likely.

Matthew has Jesus crucified by destructive forces. Pilate and Herod along with the high priests—politics and religion—conspire to cause Christ's death. Then, to be certain he is truly dead and gone, a contingent of soldiers is dispatched to guard his grave. But notice: In Matthew's presentation, the power of God is greater than any human force. The earth shakes (see Exod. 19:18; Ps. 68:8; Isa. 13:13, and elsewhere), a dazzling angel appears, and the soldiers fall down in a dead faint. Human power is always destructive—the sword, the bomb, the sophisticated missile—but God's might is the unstoppable power of Life, with a capital L.

The angel speaks to the women, as biblical angels tend to do, with a stock greeting: "Do not be afraid!" The command, though effective, is amusing considering the earthquake and the angel's appearance, which is described as "like lightning." Presumably the experience might be somewhat unsettling. Anyway, the angel recites what may be an early church creedal formula: "He is not here; for he has been raised." Please notice that the resurrection announcement always includes an emphatic statement of Christ's absence.

Then the angel hands out what is in effect an evangelical commission: "Go tell," the angel says. With great joy, the women obey the mandate; they run to tell the other disciples. But along the way they bump into the risen Christ himself. What characterizes the risen Christ's speech? Nothing; he is redundant. He merely repeats the angel's message almost word-for-word. Why is the appearance account added to Mark's original scenario? Perhaps to underscore our proper response to the resurrection: (1) the women obeyed the evangelical mandate, and (2) "they took hold of his feet, and worshiped him." Thus Matthew begins and ends his Gospel with worship. At Christ's birth the Magi bowed, and now at his rising, prostrate women bow in adoration.

The problem with preaching Matt. 28:1-10 is precisely its spectacular character. Can contemporary congregations accept as historical truth a story in which the earth quakes on cue, a bed-sheet angel suddenly appears, and a whole troop of soldiers faint all at once? Answer: Probably not. But why should preachers bother to turn a symbolic story into literal history? The earthquake and the angel and the fearful troops all serve to bring us a profound theological message—God's life-giving power is greater than our human propensity toward hostile destruction.

Matthew's Easter message is a message for our world. We live in our contending nations amid dark, devastating powers. Not only is there the dreadful prospect of nuclear death but nowadays add the Stealth bomber, the Tomahawk missile, and the bright flash of the laser sword. In a world where power has become terrifying (remember the Gulf War), Matthew declares God's greater might. Can anything stand in the way of God's purposes? Can anyone stymie God's gift of life? Not a chance, according to Matthew. His gospel message is worth preaching, which of course is our churchly task. "Go tell," the angel declared. What is our calling? We live to worship the risen Christ and tell the good news of God's great power.

Second Sunday of Easter

Lutheran	Roman Catholic	Episcopal	Common Lectionary
Acts 2:14a, 22-32	Acts 2:42-47	Acts 2:14a, 22-32	Acts 2:14a, 22-32
1 Pet. 1:3-9	1 Pet. 1:3-9	1 Pet. 1:3-9	1 Pet. 1:3-9
John 20:19-31	John 20:19-31	John 20:19-31	John 20:19-31

FIRST LESSON: ACTS 2:14a, 22-32

For Acts 2:42-47, see the Third Sunday of Easter.

Most ancient historians included speeches within their narratives. Speeches would add variety and possibly edify readers. Luke is no exception. The speeches we find in Acts are not eyewitness recollections; they are Luke's creative writing and are designed with great care. Although the speeches do summarize Luke's understanding of the gospel, they scarcely model the homiletic practices of the era; there is no solid evidence that preachers preached such sermons in the first century.

As we have already noted, most of the sermons in Acts follow much the same pattern: (1) reference to the situation at hand; (2) a summary of the gospel; (3) an appeal to Scripture; (4) an offer of salvation and a call to repentance. Our lectionaries abbreviate Peter's sermon by dropping both the reference to the situation (including the citation from Joel) and the final appeal, vv. 38-39. Thus the assigned passage begins with the kerygmatic section of the sermon, vv. 22-24 and then concludes with an appeal to Scripture, proving Jesus' messiahship, vv. 25-32. If vv. 25-32 establish Jesus as Messiah, vv. 33-36 also draw on Scripture to prove Christ's Lordship. No wonder that v. 36 will conclude that "God has made him both Lord and Messiah."

Summaries of the gospel in Luke's sermons follow much the same progressive scheme: The name of Jesus is declared, "Jesus of Nazareth" (v. 22); his ministry is described, "deeds of power, wonders, and signs" (v. 22); then his death is mentioned, "crucified and killed" (v. 23); and finally, his resurrection, "God raised him up" (v. 24). Notice that in each step of the sequence God is mentioned: God attests the named man, Jesus; God has done the wonders through him; Jesus is crucified by "the definite plan and foreknowledge of God"; and, finally, "God raised him up." Thus we get parallel actions: Human beings crucify Christ but, at the same time, it all happens by God's own design. In Luke such parallel statements are typical and are part of his incarnational theology. He will tell us that Jesus is a mighty prophet and then, in a next sentence, affirm that, in Jesus, God has visited us.

The appeal to Scripture, vv. 25-32, quotes Ps. 16:8-11 from the Septuagint (LXX). Luke, along with most other first-century Christians, accepts the tradition that David wrote the Psalms. Because Psalm 16:10 (LXX) reads, "For you will not abandon my soul to Hades," Luke has Peter explain that in using "*my* soul" David cannot be speaking of himself; after all, David is dead and buried and "his tomb is with us to this day" (v. 29). Instead, he argues, David is envisioning the promised Messiah, a descendant whom God will enthrone (Ps. 132:11). Therefore, he explains, Psalm 16 might as well read, "*He* was not abandoned to Hades" (v. 31). The appeal to Scripture is somewhat labored, but it ends with a grand declaration: "This Jesus God raised up, and of that all of us are witnesses" (v. 32).

Notice that the sermon is addressed to "Israelites" (v. 22). The audience gathered was not merely people of Jerusalem but Jews from outlying lands who were in Jerusalem during Pentecost (see 2:7-11). Yet in v. 23, Luke has Peter address his audience boldly, "this man . . . you crucified and killed." Immediately he adds, "But God raised him up." God reversed the verdict of crucifixion so that, now, we human beings may repent and acknowledge God's Messiah. By the way, we must be careful in preaching to make the "you" in the passage refer to *us* in the church lest we inadvertently fan any smoldering anti-Semitism.

The sections of the sermon in the lectionary can be preached. Admittedly, the appeal to Scripture is complicated, but its logic need not be rehearsed from the pulpit. Both sections imply a mystery of human action and divine purpose. Even the appeal to Scripture proposes that Jesus, the crucified, is in fact the promised Messiah, a son of David now enthroned by resurrection. A preacher can explore the mystery of human agency and God's design. Although we reject God's own chosen one and, indeed, nail him to a cross, God acts through our deeds and still brings about the eternal purpose, the promises of old—I will be your God and you will be my people.

Such a gospel is surely good news. In our world God's ways are flouted and the Christ ignored. Nevertheless, God will work through our dismay and still bring about the eternal purpose. The message of Luke's sermon is nothing less than the sure triumph of grace.

SECOND LESSON: 1 PETER 1:3-9

First Peter is a letter from a fairly literate Christian to Christians in rural Asia Minor. Most of those addressed seem to have been resident aliens and slaves. We don't know exactly when the letter was written, but most scholars argue for a late first-century date, though some scholars will push the letter into the early second century. The letter is attributed to the apostle Peter (v. 1) as transcribed by Silvanus (4:12), but it was common practice to compose letters as if written by some distinguished apostle—Peter or Paul or James or John.

The Christians being addressed are apparently facing persecution, and 1 Peter is written to encourage their faith. The letter is peculiar, however, because it seems to contain a separate document. Thus, a section from 1:3 to 4:11 has its own distinct measured style and content; it has an introduction, 1:3-12, and a conclusion with final exhortations and a doxology, 4:7-11. The material is concerned with the Christian life, has a sermonic style, and may have been a speech prepared for the newly baptized.

The remainder of the letter, 4:12—5:14, is much more direct in style and specific in reference. Instead of contemplating suffering, Christians are now actually being persecuted in a "fiery ordeal." Did a single author put the sections together, first quoting his own previously prepared material and then following up with sharp practical exhortation? Perhaps. Our lection, 1:3-9, is part of the introduction to the sermonic section of the letter.

The opening phrase, "Blessed be the God and Father of our Lord Jesus Christ," may well be drawn from early Christian liturgy, although it is the same as 2 Cor. 1:3. The formula "Blessed be God" occurs frequently in the Hebrew Scriptures (e.g., Ps. 66:20; 72:18) and was probably taken into Christian worship. In this case, 1 Pet. 1:3 may be a quote from a baptismal ritual. By God's mercy we have a "new birth" into "a living hope" via the resurrection of Jesus Christ. The same idea is to be found in Titus 3:5, where it is also connected with baptism. The term *new birth* may have come from Judaism or from the pagan mysteries, but it was soon taken into Christian usage. In baptism we participate ritually in the death and resurrection of Christ; we die to sin and are reborn and therefore now have an active, living hope.

What is our hope? Our hope is directly connected with God's saving purpose for all humanity. The author of 1 Peter uses the word *inheritance*, a term borrowed from the Hebrew Scriptures. Abraham was promised the land of Canaan, and his descendants regarded themselves as heirs of the promise; the land was their "inheritance" (Deut. 15:4; 19:10). Later, after the exile, the notion of inheritance was understood in less material terms, sometimes as God and sometimes as eternal life with God. Paul plays with the image of an inheritance, too, when he likens Christians to children of God: "If children, then heirs, heirs of God and joint heirs with Christ" (Rom. 8:17). Here in 1 Peter the "inheritance" seems to be the fullness of a glorified, redeemed life with God—in effect, salvation—which is reserved for us. Meanwhile we are to be faithful under the protection of God (v. 5).

As a result, we Christians can rejoice, yes, rejoice even in the midst of suffering the "various trials" of persecution (v. 6). The paradox of gladness in the midst of suffering has always been a characteristic of the Christian life. Calvin says it nicely: "There is here a certain appearance of inconsistency, in that the faithful, who exult in joy, are said at the same time to be in grief; for these are contrary affections. But that these can be felt simultaneously the faithful know from experience." We suffer, and our suffering may be utterly exhausting. Yet at the same time we are sure of God's promises and, in faith, strengthened by God's presence. Therefore, oddly enough, we can be glad and, yes, even grateful.

The idea of faith being refined like gold in fire may not be terribly exciting when we are in the midst of suffering, when our basic impulses may be formed by agony—hey, get us out of the fire! The idea of refined faith is a notion for retrospect. Afterward we may realize a gain in compassion and resiliency, both of which are components of Christian "toughness." But in the midst of trials, we can love, serve, and believe in Christ while we wait for the promise of our (not my) salvation (vv. 8-9).

The passage is packed with meaning, and, to be truthful, somewhat obscure meaning. Nowadays many Christians do not think of baptism as a new birth into a future hope, or if they do, they translate the whole idea into a kind of religious selfishness—"Oh, that will be glory for me" (too bad about you unbelievers). Nevertheless, the promise of redeemed life, a life liberated from not only psychological bedevilments but social corruptions (e.g., racism, militarism, sexism), is indeed a living hope for Christian people. As for rejoicing in trials, the passage is no doubt thinking of persecutions for faith, something not feared by most North Americans. Although we may well oppress, we are not often oppressed. Yet in this world many Christians do have a hint of what it means to cling by faith to Christ, who suffered, was crucified, and yet has been raised to glory. To some degree we can celebrate our sure hope in the midst of troubles.

GOSPEL: JOHN 20:19-31

Here are two passages that, though related, should probably produce two different sermons. The reading includes the locked room story in which Jesus appears to frightened disciples on Easter Day, vv. 19-23, and the episode in which Jesus shows up again a week later for the benefit of doubting Thomas. Following these, vv. 30-31 write a conclusion to the Gospel, or did so until chapter 21 was added by some later editor. The first of the two passages is listed in lectionaries for Pentecost. Therefore we shall focus here on the second passage, the story of doubting Thomas.

Thomas is one of "the twelve." Although there are actually only eleven disciples on hand, the Gospel uses the traditional term *twelve*. He had not been with the other disciples when the risen Christ appeared. So they told him, "We have seen the Lord." But Thomas is not easily convinced: "Unless I see the mark of the nails in his hands, and put my finger in the mark of the nails and my hand in his side, I will not believe." Strong, stubborn words indeed!

Then, a week later, the risen Jesus appears again. "A week later" indicates that the day was again "the first day of the week," a Lord's Day, the traditional time for Christian worship. But in v. 26, "a week later" may also refer to the idea of an eighth day, the first day of a new creation according to Jewish symbolism. Jesus appears in the same way as before. Although doors are locked, suddenly he stands among his disciples and once more says, "Peace be with you." The saying fulfills an earlier promise: "Peace I leave with you; my peace I give to you" (14:27). In the earlier appearance, he had spoken the same words and, in so doing, formally confers peace on the community of faith—God's good shalom.

Then Jesus turns and speaks sharply to stubborn Thomas. The words might be translated: "Take your finger, here are my hands; take your fist, jam it in my side. Quit being faithless, but be faithful!" Most of us have heard sermons on how patient Jesus is with our doubts. And some of us may even recall Paul Tillich's contention that we are probably justified by our doubts as much as by faith. Well, not here. Jesus is clearly angry. His words lash out so that brash Thomas is driven down on his knees, crying out, "My Lord and my God." The phrase is probably a liturgical confession of faith used in the early church.

So why is Jesus furious with that early-day empiricist Thomas? After all, doubts assail us all. Moreover, there's something honest about the demand to see and touch and know truth for sure. Isn't skeptical Thomas better than believers who live by blind faith and never question their convictions? Hee-haw religion may be big these days in America, but it has never been biblical; we ought to be curious about the things of God. Yet Jesus bristles at Thomas. Some scholars suppose that Jesus is peeved with Thomas's arrogance—can a mere mortal demand that God be proved before the bar of human judgment? But, again, the contention is not supported by the story.

Jesus himself offers a clue when he hands out another beatitude: "Blessed are those who have not seen and yet have come to believe." All through the Gospel of John signs are given to confirm faith. People believe on the basis of Jesus' word, and then a miraculous sign is given to establish faith fully—water into wine or the healing of a child or sight given to a blind man or the raising of Lazarus, and so forth. People see a sign and then truly believe. Does John regard the resurrection as the last great sign given? Probably. Are we now called to believe on the basis of the word alone? Thomas had heard the resurrection preached by the other disciples but refused to believe. "Blessed are those who have not seen and yet have come to believe," says Jesus.

The passage does address us twentieth-century Christians. We will never see the risen Christ. We will not poke at his wounds. We cannot pressure him to appear with dazzling signs and wonders before our rationality. Instead Christ comes to us as an Easter rumor by word of mouth—in sermons, songs, Scripture, and liturgy. We are asked to believe the good news on the basis of the word we hear and what John Calvin called "the inward testimony of the Holy Spirit" with the community. In faith, together we can proclaim, "My Lord and my God."

Is the entire Gospel of John written as a word for faith? Listen: "These [words] are written so that you may come to believe that Jesus is the Messiah, the Son of God, and that through believing you may have life in his name" (v. 31). No proofs, no wounds to scratch, no sudden appearing of a risen Christ drifting through locked doors. We can believe on the basis of the word we hear and then have life, true life, in the Spirit of the Lord.

Third Sunday of Easter

Lutheran	Roman Catholic	Episcopal	Common Lectionary
Acts 2:14a, 36-47	Acts 2:14a, 22-33	Acts 2:14a, 36-47	Acts 2:14a, 36-41
1 Pet. 1:17-21	1 Pet. 1:17-21	1 Pet. 1:17-23	1 Pet. 1:17-23
Luke 24:13-35	Luke 24:13-35	Luke 24:13-35	Luke 24:13-35

FIRST LESSON: ACTS 2:14a, 36-47

For Acts 2:14a, 22-33, see the Second Sunday of Easter.

Here we have what is actually a conclusion to Peter's Pentecost speech, vv. 36-41, and then a summary description of the common life of the early Christian community, vv. 42-47. Frequently the lectionary offers chunks of Scripture from which more than a single sermon may be preached. These two sections should probably be developed into two different sermons.

Virtually all of the speeches in Acts conclude with the offer of salvation and a call to repentance. Luke's call for repentance is based on the great reversal of the resurrection: "Jesus Christ of Nazareth, whom you crucified, whom God raised from the dead" (4:10). The word *raised* does not merely mean a rescue from death; it indicates exaltation. The Jesus whom we rejected, condemned, and put to death by capital punishment, God has enthroned as the world's Lord and Savior. In view of the new state of affairs, we had better repent and change our allegiances quickly. Peter's audience seems to sense the urgency: "What shall we do?" they ask. Their catechetical question is answered with a formula response: (1) repent; (2) be baptized for the forgiveness of sins; and (3) receive the Holy Spirit.

Then comes an exchange prompted by Ps. 78:5-8. The psalm refers to teaching children, children's children, and the children of children as yet unborn (78:5-6) so that we may be separate from "a stubborn and rebellious generation" (78:8). Peter announces that the promise of salvation is to us and to our children, meaning the many generations of our descendants. And he concludes with a sharp word of advice: "Save yourselves from this corrupt generation" (v. 40), which implies separation and a new loyalty to the Lord Christ.

17

Preaching repentance and the promise of salvation is not easy. Certainly we must not offer salvation, like a carrot on a stick, as a reward for those who are properly repentant. To do so is to turn repentance into a work: Take a dive for Jesus and we'll hand you a ticket to heaven! No, Peter's sermon begins not with a call to repent, but with a word about what God has done; God has raised up Jesus and made him Lord and Christ. Repentance is properly a response to and not a condition of salvation. In Acts as elsewhere in the Christian Scriptures, repentance is not necessarily an emotional orgy of regret, all salt tears on a sawdust trail; rather to repent is to change our whole orientation. We will no longer live to satisfy the public mind or the values of our age—even religious values. Instead we will live in a new, exciting way as citizens of Christ's new order. What is the rationale for repenting? God has raised up Jesus!

The speech concludes in v. 41 with the baptism of three thousand people. Do you suppose that the church's tendency to overestimate evangelistic conquests began with the book of Acts?

The second section of the reading, vv. 42-47, is one of several summary descriptions of the early community that can be found in Acts. They tend to rehearse the same themes. Mention of their teaching shows up in 4:2, 18 and in 5:21-28, 42. Reference to their "prayers" shows up again in 4:24-30 and 6:4-6. We learn of their "spending time together in the temple" here (2:46), but also in 3:1, 11 and 5:12, 20-25, 42. The "signs and wonders" of the apostles are recorded also in 4:16, 22, 30; 5:12; 6:8; and 7:36. We get several mentions of their "awe," of the public "favor" they win, and of the growth of the community.

The summary descriptions are not mere filler, transitions scribbled to get us from one episode to another. They are deliberately designed and repeated for a purpose. They depict the ideal church for future Christian generations. We read the descriptions and measure our congregations by their words. The summary descriptions call us to be all that we can and must be in order to continue the work of Jesus Christ, who prayed, shared, worshiped in the temple, did signs and wonders, and surely won favor with those he served.

The summary mentions "breaking bread," Luke's special way of referring to the Lord's Supper, our Eucharist. The term intends not merely ritual actions—breaking bread and pouring wine—but a full-scale meal. Although Luke wrote in the late eighties or nineties, the

Lord's Supper had not yet been truncated. The suppers were full meals ✓ marked by both solemnity and gladness; they were indeed "thanks-givings" (*eucharistia*).

Luke's reference to common property is somewhat more troubling, particularly to contemporary free-enterprise Americans. Does the book of Acts endorse communism? Isn't our free enterprise divinely approved? In Greek thinking, true friendship is displayed in sharing. According to Aristotle, "The property of friends is held in common." Sharing was also a Jewish ideal, and still is. Kinship requires radical sharing. Obviously, if we are sisters and brothers in Christ, we too are "kin." The early community shared in order to supply food and income to those in need, and the need of others clearly overruled any notion of private ownership of property—as is quite clear in the subsequent story of Ananias and Sapphira (Acts 5:1-32). More than any of the Gospels, Luke pictures Jesus again and again speaking on the dangers of wealth and the necessity of radical charity. In Acts, therefore, Luke depicts a church that lives the word of Christ. While we have neighbors who are hungry, homeless, naked, or oppressed, no property is private!

How do we preach the summaries? We hold them up as ideals and call our churches to embody them boldly.

SECOND LESSON: 1 PETER 1:17-21

The passage, though often quoted, is murky. Prior to v. 17, 1 Pet. 1:1-16 has urged morality on the basis of God's character, revealed in Jesus Christ: "You shall be holy, for I am holy." Now the author rallies a second and then a third argument for the Christian life.

First, in v. 17, the writer suggests that the God Christians pray to as "Father" (a reference to the Lord's Prayer?) is in fact the judge of the whole world. God judges people impartially on the basis of deeds done. The word *impartiality* is literally "to receive the face" and means something like our phrase "face value." Although Christians may claim a special childlike relationship to God, the Parent, the relationship earns no brownie points when it comes to judgment. God judges on the "face value" of works done. Therefore we should live our earthly lives in awe. Protestant Christians need to remember that though we are justified by grace through faith, nevertheless ultimately we will be judged by works—that is, by the works of faith. What is more, our justification by God's love does not exempt us from moral seriousness.

Now the argument shifts from the character of God to God's great redemption in Christ; the author now speaks not of God our Judge but God our Savior. Christian morality is not driven by cowering fear but is prompted by gratitude for God's great salvation. We know that we have been "ransomed" from futile patterns of living (a twentieth-century problem), not with cash down, but by the blood of Christ. Verses 18-19 are difficult. The text appears to mix metaphors—ransom and sacrifice. But the verb that the NRSV translates "ransomed" can mean merely "rescued" or "set free from," and in this verse such a general meaning may be a better translation. The blood of Christ, though precious, is not regarded as a ransom payment to secure the release of enslaved people. Instead the metaphor is the blood of sacrifice—like a sacrificial lamb without defect or blemish. The blood of sacrifice, identified with an animal's life, was evidently considered efficacious in itself. In some way, the blood of Christ has rescued us from empty, meaningless, conventional lives, "futile ways inherited from your ancestors." Through Christ our "faith and hope are set on God."

The phrase in v. 20—"He was destined before the foundation of the world, but was revealed at the end of the ages"—is probably a quotation from liturgy, perhaps from a baptismal liturgy, with which 1 Peter's audience is familiar. But it is a crucial theological notion that is also found in Ephesians and Colossians. We must never regard Jesus Christ as an emergency reaction on God's part, as if our chronic sinfulness had forced God to act in Christ. The incarnation would thus have been caused by our sin. No, God intended Christ from the "foundation of the world" and, at the right moment, revealed him to us beloved sinners.

Then 1 Peter hands out a sermon in a single sentence: "Through him [Christ] you have come to trust God, who raised him from the dead and gave him glory, so that your faith and hope are set on God" (v. 21). In a handful of words, 1 Peter has described the character of the Christian life: We trust God. Why? Because through Christ we have come to know God. God is self-giving love. Have we not been liberated by "the blood of Christ"? More, God is the lifegiver whose power raised up Jesus Christ from the dead. So God is a lifegiver and a self-giver, all in one. No wonder a Christian's hope and faith are "set on God."

The passage from 1 Peter may be difficult, but it can become a splendid sermon. Certainly we can begin by acknowledging who we are; we are children of God who pray, "Our Father." But, watch out, we must not presume on God's love. We will be judged along with everyone else on the basis of our deeds. Have we fed the hungry, clothed the naked, visited the prisoner, comforted the lonely, and so forth? Yet might not the threat of judgment plunge us into a busyness of works? No, for the power of Christ has set us free from the law of oughts and musts. We know we are liberated people. Then why should we live as Christians? Because we are grateful for God's amazing grace, that's why. The sequence of thought within the passage is practically a sermon in itself.

The passage contains an interesting phrase that we may easily overlook: The author tells us that we have been rescued from "futile ways inherited from your ancestors." He does not use the stock word *sin.* Instead he refers to aimless conventional ways of living inherited from the past. The passage may address our age in a unique manner. Again and again we find ourselves trapped in nonsensical patterns of behavior that we have inherited and uncritically adopted. What about military power in a nuclear age, for example? Have we inherited the notion that warfare can resolve human conflicts? And what about "free enterprise"? Do we suppose that we are free to profit without much concern for those on the bottom of the economic heap? Maybe a "futile way" is the terrible clutch of the empty past upon our lives. Thank God that in Christ's good grace we are freed to live our lives in a new way!

GOSPEL: LUKE 24:13-35

The story of the Emmaus road has been a favorite with preachers for centuries. In a way the story is easy to preach, for it has a clear plot with defined episodes. Yet the story has nuances that can be missed as well as profound meanings for our life together.

The story begins with two discouraged people walking down a road. Most sermons refer to them as two men, only one of whom is named, Cleopas. But the two could be a woman and a man; Cleopas might be the "Clopas" mentioned in John 19:25—"Mary the wife of Clopas." As they walk along, they are rehashing all that had happened—the trial, the cruelty, the cross, the death. The word the NRSV translates "discussing" is a word often used to describe rabbinic question-counterquestion discourse. Then the risen Lord Jesus joins them, "but their eyes were kept from recognizing him." God's own special sleight of hand seems to have confused their vision. So now there are three people walking the seven-mile stretch of road to Emmaus.

"What are you talking about?" the stranger asks. Cleopas answers saying in effect, "Are you the only one who hasn't heard what's been going on in Jerusalem lately?" The two disciples begin to tell about Jesus—"a prophet mighty in deed and word." Perhaps they are alluding to the promise of a messianic prophet in Deut. 18:18 and again in Mal. 4:5. "Our chief priests and leaders handed him over" to death, they explain. (Notice that Luke lays the blame for Jesus' death on Jewish leaders, not on the people or on the Roman politicos.) "We had thought he was the one to redeem Israel," they explain pathetically.

Now the story shifts and an extra story of the women at the tomb is pieced (somewhat clumsily) into the narrative. "Some women of our group" came up with an astounding report. They said they found the tomb empty and, from a vision of angels, heard news that Christ was alive. The disciples checked the report and found the tomb empty; but "we didn't see him," they said. So they refused to believe the good news, perhaps because it was broadcast by women. What use is an idle rumor against the brute fact of death?

Suddenly Jesus interrupts them, saying in effect, "You blockheads!" How slow they are to credit all that prophecy had written: "Was it not necessary that the Messiah should suffer these things and then enter into his glory?" he asks—a very Lukan notion. Then of all things Jesus stands in the Emmaus road and preaches a sermon: "beginning with Moses and all the prophets, he interpreted to them things about himself in all the scriptures." Jewish synagogue preaching expounded ("interpreted") texts from the Torah (Moses) and haftarah (prophets), a practice that was probably taken over in early Christian communities. Right in the middle of the road, Jesus stops and preaches a small-scale sermon.

As they come near the village, Jesus acts as if he were going on farther. But they persuade him to stay with them, and he joins them at the dinner table. Then, with ritual solemnity, Jesus "took bread, blessed and broke it, and gave it to them." Luke is using formula words associated with the celebration of the Eucharist, the Lord's Supper. "Then their eyes were opened and they recognized him." After Jesus vanishes, the two say to each other, "Were not our hearts burning while he was talking to us on the road, while he was opening the scriptures to us?" So they get up, race back to Jerusalem, and describe to other disciples how the risen Lord was known to them "in the breaking of the bread," a term Luke repeatedly uses in Acts to describe the Lord's Supper.

Ask yourself why Luke would tell a story so that preaching the word and celebrating a sacrament stand out so baldly? Why would Luke want his audience to recognize these actions—"Look there, Jesus is preaching a sermon," "See, now he is conducting the Eucharist. Surely the Lord Christ is risen among us!"

How difficult it is these days to shore up resurrection faith. We rally Bible passages, but either the passages are farfetched, fairy-tale stuff, full of cracked tombs and angel emcees, or they leave us asking questions: What did the risen Jesus look like? What did the disciples experience? The Bible does not answer our questions. Perhaps we hope for a vision of Christ alive to settle the matter once and for all; but visions are in short supply in our crass world. As for appealing to the fact of the church after so many centuries, the argument is somehow unconvincing, perhaps because the church is often trivial and unsatisfying. But the ministry of Jesus Christ is still happening. The gospel is preached, people are forgiven, and bread is shared at table. The ministry of Christ continues in the midst of our sinful, hung up, helpless, inane, self-righteous humanity. Surely the work of Christ is animated by his own living power, for if it depended on us, it wouldn't be.

Here is a problem for preachers. As a preacher, can you design a sermon so that as you tell the Emmaus road story your congregation will realize Christ is preaching a sermon and conducting the Lord's Supper? Can you preach so that suddenly your people will know Christ lives and still speaks in preaching and is present in the breaking of bread?

Fourth Sunday of Easter

Lutheran	Roman Catholic	Episcopal	Common Lectionary
Acts 6:1-9, 7:2a, 51-60	Acts 2:14a, 36-41	Acts 6:1-9, 7:2a, 51-60	Acts 2:42-47
1 Pet. 2:19-25	1 Pet. 2:20-25	1 Pet. 2:19-25	1 Pet. 2:19-25
John 10:1-10	John 10:1-10	John 10:1-10	John 10:1-10

FIRST LESSON: ACTS 6:1-9; 7:2a, 51-60

For Acts 2:14a, 36-41, 42-47 see the Third Sunday of Easter.

If you insist on accusing your congregation of murder and their respected ancestors of being killers too, you can look for a violent reaction to your sermon. Stephen's sermon was not exactly politic. He was speedily martyred.

The episode begins with an installation of new church officers. The apostles—"the twelve"—were overloaded by administrative demands. The early church had a kind of meals-on-wheels program that apparently involved daily food distribution to the hungry. In usual Jewish practice, regularly dependent persons received a food allowance weekly, while "strangers" were taken a food tray day by day. Probably the early church could not rely on Jewish welfare and therefore was operating hand to mouth.

In any event, the food program occasions conflict between local Aramaic-speaking members, "Hebrews," and Greek-speaking members, "Hellenists," who have more recently moved to Jerusalem. Hellenist widows are not receiving their needed food allowances. To resolve matters, the apostles suggest the election of additional persons, "the seven," to administer the program; the word for "wait on tables" (v. 2) is *diakonein,* from which we get our word *deacon.* The decision is not elitist, as if preaching and praying are more important than lesser works like charitable food distribution. The sudden rapid growth of the Christian community has merely made a more complex administrative structure necessary. Seven persons of "good standing" are therefore chosen, among them Stephen and Philip. They are people "full of wisdom and the Spirit." The community installs them in office by prayer and the laying on of hands (see Num. 27:18-23). The new administrative pattern worked: "The word of God continued to spread; the number of the disciples increased in Jerusalem" (v. 7). So far so good.

But then, inexplicably, there is trouble. Evidently Stephen is much more than a program person; he "did great wonders and signs among the people" (v. 8). As a result, Stephen stirs up opposition from a rather right-wing Jewish synagogue, the "synagogue of the Freedmen," which seems to have had a congregation of diaspora Jews who were apt to be somewhat overzealous. They instigate a confrontation, saying, "We have heard him speak blasphemous words against Moses and God"— that is, against the law and the temple (vv. 11, 13). Stephen is hauled before the council much as Jesus was. Judaism had a long tradition of martyr's speeches (see 2 Macc. 7:14-19; 4 Macc. 5-12), and in good company Stephen launches a rhetorical defense: "Brothers and fathers, listen to me . . ."

The lectionary selection skips most of Stephen's rather lengthy address in order to focus on his concluding words. The speech is almost certainly composed by Luke, perhaps drawing on some sort of source; it articulates Luke's view of salvation history. In the body of the speech, Stephen speaks of God's generous promises to Abraham and Joseph and Moses, of the covenant law and the building of the temple. He rehearses biblical history from Abraham to Solomon, telling a story of God and Israel. Of course, he also picks up the theme of Israel's chronic rejection of God; recounting a parallel record of the people's disobedience and violent disrespect. Then boldly he phrases his conclusion.

He begins with some scriptural name-calling—"stiff-necked" (Deut. 10:16), "uncircumcised in heart and ears" (Exod. 33:3)—and then proceeds to accuse the council of opposing the Holy Spirit as their ancestors did (v. 51). Their ancestors, Stephen points out, killed the prophets, prophets who predicted the coming of "the Righteous One" (v. 52). The theme of killing prophets is scriptural (e.g., see 1 Kings 19:10-14; Neh. 9:26; 2 Chron. 36:16). Finally he accuses them of breaking the law of God: "You are the ones that received the law as ordained by angels, and yet you have not kept it" (v. 53). Later Jewish tradition supposed that the law of God was transmitted to Moses by angels (see Gal. 3:19).

How did Stephen's sermon go over? "When they heard these things, they became enraged and ground their teeth at Stephen" (v. 54). Whereupon, of all things, Stephen, gazing up, spots a vision of the risen Jesus at the right hand of God's glory: "Look," he exclaims, "I see the heavens opened and the Son of Man standing at the right hand of God!" (v. 56). The term "Son of Man" is seldom used outside the Gospels. Here it echoes Luke 22:69, Jesus' words at his trial, "from now on the Son of Man will be seated at the right hand of the power of God." The vision is even more upsetting; and, as if to demonstrate Stephen's accusations, the council "covered their ears," refusing to hear. They rush Stephen and haul him out of the city (Deut. 17:2-5) to be stoned, the traditional penalty for blasphemy (Lev. 24:10-23). Note the brief mention of Paul, a.k.a. Saul, in v. 58.

Stephen's death recalls Jesus' crucifixion: "Lord Jesus," he cries, "receive my spirit," matching Jesus' commendation in Luke 23:46. Then he cries out in a loud voice (Luke 23:46), "Lord, do not hold this sin against them," and dies. His last words remind us of Jesus' "Father forgive them" (Luke 23:34). Why has Luke drawn obvious parallels between Christ's death and Stephen's martyrdom? Because structurally they are similar. In each case people were trying to silence the word of God, and in each case God's power was greater. After martyrdom, the word of God, a word of forgiveness and renewal, spreads even more rapidly and efficaciously.

A cruel story is told of a missionary who preached on the saving power of martyrdom. His audience was moved and, to prove his point, murdered him. Whereupon his sermon came true and they were all converted. The story may be harsh, but it reflects Luke's own sure conviction. "Jesus whom you crucified, God has raised up"—such is Luke's credo. Surely Stephen is raised, and his death confronts his accusers with the truth of God. As a result, the church grows. Eventually Stephen's death will transform Saul of Tarsus into the apostle Paul.

SECOND LESSON: 1 PETER 2:19-25

Sometimes the Bible can be irritating. Here is some advice for slaves on proper behavior. But the whole question of slavery is never raised. Doesn't the gospel imply a liberation from enslavement? How could 1 Peter accept such a dreadful social institution? Perhaps 1 Peter, along with most of the Christian writings, assumes an early transformation of the social order, "a new heaven and a new earth," soon to appear with the coming of Christ. A soon-to-be-changed status quo is no status quo at all. So 1 Peter speaks of slavery on a "meanwhile" basis, knowing that soon it will be swept away in God's new order. Of course, we should not tolerate enslavement simply because it seems to be accepted by 1 Peter and therefore is in the Bible. Fundamentalism is not only heresy, it can be a socially repressive heresy!

The lectionary skips v. 18, the embarrassing direct reference to slavery, hoping thereby to give the passage a more general reference. Though most slave owners treated their people decently, some were irascible and some few were even sadistic. Slaves, who were evidently the majority of 1 Peter's congregation, were not merely laborers; some held positions of fiscal responsibility as managers or accountants, others were involved in what we would term "service professions." But on occasion even responsible slaves were beaten. First Peter does not romanticize slavery: If you are beaten for doing wrong, what credit do you get? he asks (v. 20a). But then he reverses the situation: "If you endure when you do right and suffer for it, you have God's approval" (v. 20b). Why is righteous suffering approved? Because Christ suffered unjustly—"He committed no sin, and no deceit was found in his mouth," says 1 Peter, loosely quoting Isa. 53:9.

First Peter then holds up Christ as an example of innocent, patient suffering. "When he was abused, he did not return abuse; when he suffered, he did not threaten; but he entrusted himself to the one who judges justly" (v. 23; see Isa. 53:7). If the words are a counsel of compliant self-abasement, they are dreadful. "Put up and shut up" has never been gospel! On the other hand, we can receive the words in two ways: (1) as a call to brave endurance in God's righteous cause; and (2) as a call to the nonviolent power of suffering love, as, for example, in the valiant life of Martin Luther King, Jr.

Now suddenly 1 Peter does broaden his discussion: "He himself bore our sins in his body on the cross, so that, free from sins, we might live for righteousness; by his wounds you have been healed" (v. 24). The verse has been central to Christian proclamation for centuries. Is the verse alluding to a scapegoat on which the sins of Israel were cast (Leviticus 16)? Probably not. Instead the phrase "bore our sins" seems to mean bore the consequence of our sins. Christ died the death we deserve, and we now live the righteous life he intends. The reference to Christ's wounds, drawn from Isa. 53:5, no doubt brings to mind his scourging. Beaten slaves could identify with a Lord who was also beaten. The final verse, v. 25, introduces the image of the shepherd, an image prompted no doubt by Isa. 53:6 and perhaps influenced by the notion of God as the shepherd of Israel.

Although preachers may be tempted, 1 Peter does not lend itself to a discussion of human suffering per se. A nearby "Missionary Church" has a sign in front that reads, "Suffering Is the Soil in Which Faith Grows." But human pain is overrated; it may neither edify nor ennoble; it may in fact embitter. Our suffering may not even put us in touch with the suffering of the Lord. No, the issue is the unjust suffering of the righteous. Just as Christ, though innocent, suffered and thereby set us free, so our suffering in good courage may be efficacious.

? We must be careful in preaching 1 Peter that we do not piously endorse repression. But we can call people to bravery and love in the midst of suffering, following in the way of Jesus Christ.

The passage from 1 Peter has probably been chosen to align with John 10:1-10, the good shepherd passage, but the reference to the shepherd in 1 Pet. 2:25 is not much more than a tag-line afterthought.

GOSPEL: JOHN 10:1-10

The image of Jesus as the good shepherd has long been a favorite in the church. He shows up in stained glass with a lost sheep slung over his shoulder. He is sung in hymns: "The King of Love My Shepherd Is." Although the image may seem remote in modern urban settings, it still has power.

In John 10 Jesus provides us with a picture of the sheepfold and the shepherd, and then in vv. 7-16 he provides at least four different interpretations of the images. Some scholars label the picture a parable, and others, an allegory. Certainly the passage seems to function allegorically; though the image is static, like a still life, different aspects of it are interpreted.

At the outset, we should spot the "I am" (*ego eimi*) with which many of the Johannine allegories begin ("I am the bread of life," "I am the light of the world," "I am the true vine," etc.). The words are the divine name: God spoke to Moses from the burning bush, announcing, "I am who I am" (Exod. 3:14). In the Gospel of John, again and again Jesus speaks a mysterious "I am." Here are two such declarations: "I am the gate" (v. 7); "I am the good shepherd" (v. 11).

The shepherd image is scarcely original with Jesus. Shepherd is a frequent metaphor in the Hebrew Scriptures. In Gen. 49:24, God is the shepherd of Israel. God is a shepherd in Psalm 23 and in Ps. 78:52, where Israel is God's "flock." Good leaders and kings are those who, like Joshua, "shall lead them out and bring them in, so that the congregation of the Lord may not be like sheep without a shepherd" (Num. 27:17). Of course the great passage is Ezekiel 34, in which God condemns the plundering shepherds of Israel and in turn promises to be a good shepherd. Preachers should read Ezekiel's chapter before trying to interpret John 10:1-10.

Jesus seems to be picturing a farmer's fold that is fenced around and has only one doorway or sheepgate. From the image he develops two or possibly three meanings. (1) The shepherd enters by the gate. Thieves and bandits climb over the fence to get at the sheep. (The word for bandit was also used for popular revolutionaries.) (2) The gate leads out to life-giving pasture when the sheep follow the shepherd. Thieves and bandits capture sheep to kill them (as sacrifices?). (3) The sheep recognize the voice of the shepherd, who in turn knows them each by name.

After painting the picture, Jesus announces surprisingly, "I am the gate." He contrasts his intimate, life-giving concern for the sheep with those bandits who would plunder the fold and destroy the sheep. Did Jesus have the scribes and Pharisees in mind, or perhaps the temple priesthood? Again and again God's people have been misled, from biblical times to Jonestown's mass suicide. Even in our own day there are TV shepherds who may best be described as bandits. Jesus, by contrast, is the gate to salvation; he lets sheep out to graze green pastures. The test: Does the gate lead to life or to death?

Then in vv. 11-16 (which are not part of the lection) Jesus abruptly switches the metaphor: "I am the good shepherd," he says, meaning the ideal model of what shepherds should be. Again he offers two interpretations: (1) The good shepherd knows his sheep and will lay down his life for them. At night he may sleep stretched across the gateway. He does not leave sheep unprotected when wolves come, as a hired hand might do. (2) The good shepherd will gather all his sheep into one great ecumenical flock under one shepherd—himself.

The passage is somewhat awkward to preach: Are we to picture a shepherd or a sheepgate? The images seem to merge in the first ten verses. Preachers will probably picture the good shepherd. He knows his sheep and they recognize his voice as they hear it in sermons, hymns, instruction, and so forth. Christ speaks with love and seeks to set us free for life. But there are still false prophets ("Keep those cards and contributions coming") and there are still cults and causes that promise salvation but in the end destroy us. What's the true test? Abundant life!

Fifth Sunday of Easter

Lutheran	Roman Catholic	Episcopal	Common Lectionary
Acts 17:1-15	Acts 6:1-7	Acts 17:1-15	Acts 7:55-60
1 Pet. 2:4-10	1 Pet. 2:4-9	1 Pet. 2:1-10	1 Pet. 2:2-10
John 14:1-12	John 14:1-12	John 14:1-14	John 14:1-14

FIRST LESSON: ACTS 17:1-15

For Acts 6:1-7, 7:55-60, see the Fourth Sunday of Easter.

The lectionary passage might be titled "A Tale of Two Cities." Paul is forced to leave Thessalonica but is welcomed in Beroea. The passage is a study in contrasts. Paul's missionary enterprise generally meets with Jewish opposition, but not always.

The story begins with Paul and Silas traveling about a hundred miles from Philippi to Thessalonica, "where there was a synagogue of the Jews." Presumably Paul works most days at his trade in order to pay his way. Nevertheless, on three consecutive Sabbath days, he shows up in the synagogue and, arguing from the Scriptures, announces Jesus as the Christ: "This is the Messiah, Jesus whom I am proclaiming to you" (v. 3). Notice that Paul's argument is similar to the preaching of the risen Christ as reported in Luke 24:26 and 24:46, namely, the necessity of the Messiah's suffering and rising. In other words, the scandal of the Christian faith is always a crucified Christ. Paul apparently launches his argument from the prophetic writings (Luke 24:27), possibly from the Servant Songs in second Isaiah or from the "passion" Psalms (22 and 69) as well as Maccabean writings, all of which seem to have been used in early Christian interpretation. We are not told.

Some of Paul's audience was persuaded, including a number of "devout Greeks" and "not a few of the leading women" (v. 4). The support of prominent women is mentioned several times in Acts 16–18 and twice in this passage. Lydia, an affluent dealer in purple goods (an early-day Dior?), opens her home to the missionaries (16:40). A woman is also among the converts in Athens (17:34), and later Priscilla is featured in the role of a supporter and teacher (18:2, 18, 26). Was the leadership of women a feature of the Lukan church? Possibly.

Although some hearers were persuaded, many were not. According to the story, Jews, out of jealousy, got some street-smart "ruffians" to stir up a mob that "set the city in an uproar" (v. 5). Searching for Paul and Silas, the mob attacks Jason's house, dragging out "Jason and some believers." Jason's name drops into the story without introduction; we can conclude that he provided hospitality for the two missionaries during their stay in the city because the mob was hoping to find Paul and Silas in his house. The crowd hauls Jason before the local magistrates and, of all things, blames him and the apostles for the riot they themselves have incited: "These people who have been turning the world upside down have come here also, and Jason has entertained them as guests" (vv. 6-7). By "world" they are undoubtedly referring to the Roman Empire. The Jewish leaders then add a more insidious accusation: "They are all acting contrary to the decrees of the emperor, saying that there is another king named Jesus." The accusation is odd coming from Jews who supposedly affirm no king but God! Although Jason is released on bail, the disturbance is effective; it chases Paul and Silas out of town that night and on to Beroea.

Jews in Beroea are nobler; they welcome Paul's preaching eagerly and study the Scriptures with care every day. As a result many of them believe, "including not a few Greek women and men of high standing" (v. 12). But the opposition is determined; Jews from Thessalonica, hearing of Paul's success in Beroea, come over to incite the crowds. So again Paul is hustled out of town and as far as Athens, with Silas and Timothy to follow later (vv. 14-15).

Luke has deliberately chosen homiletic language with talk of king Jesus and "turning the world upside down." Notice that our Christian faith is implicitly subversive: If Christ is our risen Lord, he demotes all earthly loyalties. Perhaps the phrase "Christian patriotism," in spite of our all-American flag waving, is ultimately an outright contradiction in terms. While Luke views the accusations against Paul as trumped up, ironically the accusers may have grasped the true implications of Christian faith. Note that our risen Lord, the Messiah King, is the crucified one who was accused, scourged, and nailed helplessly to a cross. Was his death necessary? Yes. Not only does his death earn mercy for us all, but it displays what Paul labeled the foolish impotence of God (1 Corinthians 1), the only kind of power Christians can properly celebrate. We share in God's power when, like Paul, we are pursued or when, like hospitable Jason, we are charged with insurrection.

During the Sundays of Easter, we celebrate not so much life over death but the raising up of the condemned, crucified, battered Christ to the right hand of God. Indeed, his resurrection does turn worldly values upside down.

Now, a word of caution: Many of the passages from Acts that are listed in the lectionary involve Jewish opposition. But preachers must be careful in speaking of the Jews and of their opposition to early Christian evangelists. Anti-Semitism is clearly in the Christian Scriptures, whether we like to admit it or not; and it is also the shame of most Christian congregations. After the Holocaust, all Christian people must plead for mercy. So we will speak of the people of Thessalonica, or, better, we will broaden the biblical text to refer to the inevitable opposition that comes from us sinners who defend our status quo.

SECOND LESSON: 1 PETER 2:4-10

The *New Yorker* magazine publishes examples of out-of-control metaphor under the heading "Block That Metaphor." When you read the second chapter of 1 Peter, you do worry over the metaphors. In vv. 2-3, Jesus is pure, spiritual milk for "newborn" Christians, and then in the next verse he is a living stone, in fact the cornerstone for a temple made out of Christian stones. Then before you know it, 1 Peter is talking about a "chosen race, a royal priesthood, a holy nation." Block that metaphor indeed!

Verse 4 begins with "Come to him," a phrase drawn from the LXX version of Ps. 34:5, which reads, "Come to him to be enlightened." But then 1 Peter introduces the image of "a living stone," "living" because Christ is risen. The image is biblical, drawn from Ps. 118:22, "The stone that the builders rejected has become the chief cornerstone," and Isa. 28:16, "See, I am laying in Zion a foundation stone, a tested stone, a precious cornerstone, a sure foundation." The notion of the rejected stone was a favorite early Christian image (e.g., Acts 4:11) that shows up even in the Synoptic Gospels on the lips of Jesus (Mark 12:10). Notice that in 1 Peter the stone is not merely rejected by a recalcitrant Israel but is refused by the human race—"mortals."

The beauty of the stone image is that it connects with the picture of a building. So 1 Peter turns his Christian audience into "living stones" as well; "let yourselves be built into a spiritual house." The author is using the term *house* for a temple, a house of God. Again the image is familiar; it is used by Paul (1 Cor. 3:16-17; 6:19; 2 Cor. 6:16) and is also found developed in Eph. 2:21. Is Christ the foundation stone on which the temple of the Christian community is built, or is he the keystone that holds walls together? Scholars have busily argued the issue. We need not. But do see that Christianity does have a slight anti–church-building bias. Christians regard the community, a community of the Spirit built on Christ, as their true house of worship.

Notice that 1 Peter shifts the metaphor somewhat in v. 5: Not only are we "living stones" built into a temple, but we are also a priesthood within the temple offering "spiritual sacrifices." Early Christians rejected any notion of offering actual sacrifices; God requires not sacrifice but love and justice and outgoing charity. The Reformers often spoke of a "sacrifice of praise and thanksgiving." First Peter would have approved the phrase but added ethical living as well, all under the rubric of spiritual sacrifices.

Suddenly 1 Peter starts quoting his sources from the Hebrew Scriptures; first, Isa. 28:18 in v. 6, then Ps. 118:22 in v. 7, and finally Isa. 8:14-15, "A stone that makes them stumble, and a rock that makes them fall," in v. 8. Notice that Christ, "the living stone," becomes an obstruction to those "who do not believe." "They stumble," says 1 Peter, "because they disobey the word, as they were destined to do." The author is not a dedicated Calvinist, playing around with a notion of double predestination; he lived in the first or early second century and not in the sixteenth century. But 1 Peter does believe that all human affairs are held within the mighty saving purposes of God.

Finally 1 Peter heaps up metaphors in a kind of coda: "you are a chosen race, a royal priesthood, a holy nation, God's own people." The metaphors, perhaps drawn from Exod. 19:6 and Isa. 43:20-21, stress both separation and function. If we are chosen, it is not because we are attractive or morally hot stuff or because God loves us more than anyone else (even unbelievers!). We are chosen to "proclaim the mighty acts of [God] who called you out of darkness into . . . light." Then 1 Peter drops in what appears to be a garbled quote from Hosea, perhaps 2:23, saying that while once we were "no people," now in mercy we are "God's people." Please observe that all the metaphors are corporate and instrumental. Although North American religion may revel in being personal and heartfelt, here in 1 Peter we run into a different understanding. Christian faith involves a community, thus "race," "nation," "priesthood." At the same time, Christianity does not exist for its own sake. We may be "God's own people," but we have been chosen for a purpose.

When confronted with a batch of metaphors, preachers will be wise to begin with an act of theological translation: Although rejected by the world, the risen Christ has gathered us into a new-order community, called to proclaim God's wonderful liberating power, a power that has liberated us. The theological structure underlying the metaphors will offer a sermon design that then can be reimaged in a contemporary way.

GOSPEL: JOHN 14:1-12

Although the passage is filled with familiar words—"In my Father's house there are many dwelling places," "I am the way and the truth and the life," "I am in the Father and the Father is in me"—meanings are hard to come by; the passage is very difficult. Structurally the sequence of ideas is easy enough to follow: v. 1 calls disciples to courage and faith, faith in God and faith in Jesus; vv. 2-3 speak of Christ's going away, coming again, and providing a place for his disciples; vv. 4-6 contain a discussion of "the way"; followed in vv. 7-11 by a meditation on the claim "I am in the Father and the Father is in me." In a way, vv. 2-4 offer grounds for courage, and vv. 6-11 give the basis of faith.

The idea of a final speech was something of a literary convention in biblical times. John strings together a farewell speech for Jesus that begins in the middle of chapter 13, continues through chapter 16, and is concluded with a formal prayer in chapter 17. Thereafter the story of the passion commences. Thus John 14:1-11 should be read in the light of the start of the discourse in 13:31-38. Judas has suddenly left the table on his way to betray the Lord. Therefore the "hour" of Christ's being "lifted up" has begun. Jesus speaks solemnly: "Now the Son of Man has been glorified." He tells his disciples, "Little children, I am with you only a little longer." When brash Peter asks, "Where are you going?" Jesus replies, "Where I am going, you cannot follow me now; but you will follow afterward." Where is Christ going? He is being lifted up to the "Father" in glory (see 8:12-30, where much the same language is used).

Then, to still the fears of his disciples, Jesus says, "In my Father's house there are many dwelling places." The word translated "dwelling places" is not "mansions" as in the King James Version, but it could be phrased "rest stops" or even "houselets." Possibly the verse is related to Deut. 1:29-33, which pictures God "on the way," going before the children of Israel to locate camping places for them. But more likely the passage is drawing on the idea of dwellings with God, a notion found in some intertestamental literature. First Enoch 71:16, for example, reads: "All those who walk in your ways . . . have their dwelling and inheritance with you and they will not be separated from you in all eternity." Although Christians have read the words in John as an assurance of heavenly housing for the dead, many scholars are doubtful because (1) John has virtually no interest in the hereafter, and (2) references to Christ's coming again are usually promises of the Paraclete (14:15-17). Could John 14:2 therefore refer metaphorically to the community of the Spirit, the Johannine community, that will be created by Christ's death and resurrection? Perhaps. Nevertheless, because the words follow an announcement of Christ's glorification (13:31-32), they probably mean to be with Christ and to share his glory. The emphasis here is on not space or dwelling places—such language is figurative—but oneness with Christ and therefore with the "Father."

The other phrase, "I am the way and the truth and the life," is equally difficult. In Christian circles the phrase has become something of a slogan. But what exactly do the words mean? Some scholars suppose that the idea of a "way" is drawn from proto-Gnostic thinking, that is, a secret way to salvation for initiates. But the supposition is unwarranted; does not Ps. 86:11 read, "Teach me your way, O Lord, that I may walk in your truth"? Jesus has certainly spoken previously of truth (8:32, 40-46) and even more often of life (chapters 5, 6, and 11). Here he draws the terms together. The "I am" (*ego eimi*) is significant as an echo of the divine name. By "the way" Jesus presumably means a way to renewed life through the truth of his words.

Even more difficult are Jesus' claims of oneness with God that follow in vv. 7-11. We must be cautious. The Gospel of John is not venturing ontological statements having to do with the nature of Christ. The oneness between Jesus and "the Father" is a singleness of purpose as well as child-parental affection; John is not commenting on Jesus' supposed divine-human nature. In John, Jesus is the Word of God, and therefore his message is God's message, word for word. Moreover, the life Christ imparts is life from God. Thus it is quite appropriate to say, "I am in the Father and the Father is in me"—namely, the

"Father's" life and truth and love. Although the language sounds like identity talk, it rests on a conviction of "through." God speaks and acts through Christ, gives life through Christ, and, conversely, through Jesus Christ is a way to fulfillment in God.

Because the passage is so complex, it is difficult to preach. Each sentence seems to demand a separate explanatory sermon. But maybe it will help to remember that the passage is addressed to us, namely, to disciples who are trying to make a go of it in the world with Christ gone away. We are both frightened and doubtful. What is Christ's word to us? "I go to prepare a place for you"—someday we will live in the presence of the God in Christ Jesus. Meanwhile, how do we live? We live as people of the Way. We cling to the truth in Christ's words and share new life in the Spirit. So, for goodness' sake, let not our hearts be troubled!

Sixth Sunday of Easter

Lutheran	Roman Catholic	Episcopal	Common Lectionary
Acts 17:22-31	Acts 8:5-8, 14-17	Acts 17:22-31	Acts 17:22-31
1 Pet. 3:15-22	1 Pet. 3:15-18	1 Pet. 3:8-18	1 Pet. 3:13-22
John 14:15-21	John 14:15-21	John 15:1-8	John 14:15-21

FIRST LESSON: ACTS 17:22-31

The lectionary has limited the reading from Acts to Paul's speech on Mars Hill. But congregations will need to picture Athens in order to understand the speech. Thus preachers may wish to read or, perhaps better, summarize vv. 16-21 as a preface to the lection. Likewise, preachers may wish to read vv. 32-33, which conclude the speech.

Athens, when Paul visited, was a city of around five thousand persons. A tourist attraction, the city was famous for its festivals and culture. As a "university town," Athens was also known for its intellectual curiosity. Wandering the streets, Paul spots statuary—"the city was full of idols." So Paul preaches; he speaks in a synagogue on the Sabbath and in the marketplace, the agora, on weekdays. His speaking draws a crowd, including Epicurean and Stoic philosophers. Some, probably Epicureans, react with scorn, "What's this babbler talking about?"; others, with Stoic indifference, "He seems to be a proclaimer of foreign divinities," which was the accusation once leveled against Socrates. Parenthetically, Luke tells us that they had mistaken Paul's preaching of *Jesus* and the *resurrection* (*anastasin*) as a reference to two gods!

In any event, they haul Paul off to the Areopagus, saying, "May we know what this new teaching is . . . ? It sounds rather strange to us, so we would like to know what it means." Some scholars suppose that Paul's speech is a courtroom defense; that he is seized in the agora and taken before the town council. But Luke does not appear to be describing a trial. Instead, he observes, "Now all the Athenians . . . would spend their time in nothing but telling or hearing something new" (v. 21). Then the speech begins.

Most scholars regard Paul's address on Mars Hill as a Lukan creation, perhaps modeled after philosophical public addresses he had read. Certainly the style, vocabulary, and subject matter are quite alien to the

Pauline epistles. Missing are Paul's major themes—justification, the law, God's wrath, faith, a theology of the cross, and so forth. The speech Luke reports is not nearly as apocalyptic as the actual Paul. If the speech is not an actual address by the apostle, what exactly is it? Here Luke offers us a model of apologetic missionary preaching. The speech uses Greek forms of thought, cleverly connecting them to the Christian message of repentance.

Paul begins by ingratiating himself with his audience: "Athenians, I see that you are very religious." Readers will recall that Paul was distressed by the number of idols he saw when walking through the city (v. 16) and will sense that there may be a touch of irony in his words. Paul claims that among the many "objects of worship" in the city, he saw an altar inscribed "To an unknown God." Scholars have found no evidence for such an altar in Athens. But evidently there were altars inscribed to "the unknown Gods of Asia, Africa . . . ," with "unknown" meaning unacknowledged in Athens. So Paul is probably employing a little homiletic license. But the gambit probably worked: "What therefore you worship as unknown, this I proclaim to you."

Then Paul proceeds to articulate a kind of "natural theology." "The God who made the world [kosmos] and everything in it . . . does not live in shrines made by human hands." Greek thought often referred to God as "the maker," and Stoic philosophers pooh-poohed the mere idea that God could be boxed up in religious buildings. Paul continues: "nor is [God] served by human hands, as though [God] needed anything." God is a giver who supplies all our needs but needs nothing. Again, though the idea is implicit in Jewish thought, it is a familiar notion in Greek philosophy. "From one ancestor, [God] made all nations to inhabit the whole earth," Paul argues, and adds that God "allotted the times of their existence and the boundaries of the places where they would live." Is Paul, though thinking of the first Adam, appealing to some popular idea of a primal man? Perhaps. Scholars have debated the meaning of "times" and "boundaries"—do the words refer to seasons or epochs or continents or what? In a general way, however, the meaning is clear.

Now the speech turns toward matters of human destiny: Human beings were created "so that they would search for God." Although the Bible has phrases such as "Seek the Lord," which imply moral earnestness, Paul is probably hinting at an intellectual quest, which would be more than acceptable to philosophers in attendance. But the human search for God is matched by a divine nearness: "[God] is not far from each one of us." We "live and move and have our being" in God, says Paul, citing a Stoic philosopher. Then he adds, "Even some of your own poets have said, 'For we too are his offspring.'" Notice that throughout the speech Paul is enunciating Jewish-Christian ideas, but doing so in the popular language of Greek poetry and philosophy. Does Luke want us to admire Paul's shrewd missionary strategy? Probably.

The beginning of Paul's speech would have had his audience nodding with a degree of approval; he has demonstrated thoughtfulness and some familiarity with serious philosophical concerns. So far so good. But now, cleverly, Paul turns from God the Creator to God the Judge: "Since we are God's offspring, we ought not to think that the deity is like gold, or silver, or stone, an image formed by the art and imagination of mortals." The logic is stunning: If we, living beings, are God's offspring, then presumably God is also a living being. Therefore God should not be represented in inanimate stone or metal idols. Remember how Paul called the Athenians "very religious," even though he was dismayed by their idols?

Suddenly Paul announces a new human state of affairs. Previously, he says, God has overlooked epochal human ignorance, but now God "commands all people everywhere to repent." In a town where "knowing" is valued and "ignorance" is greeted with scorn, Paul has urged the populace to repent of their ignorant idolatry. The last sentence of Paul's speech becomes quite specific: God "has fixed a day on which he will have the world judged in righteousness by a man whom he has appointed, and of this he has given assurance to all by raising him from the dead." Here Paul refers to a general resurrection, a judgment day, and the resurrection of Jesus Christ, though avoiding the specific name. Well, the speech was going well until Paul suddenly talked Christian.

What was the reaction to talk of the resurrection? Some, probably the Epicureans, scoffed, while others, no doubt Stoics, said good-bye politely, "We will hear you again about this." Don't call us, we'll call you. There is an old gag about two signs. One sign reads, "This Way to God"; the other sign has, "This Way to Lectures about God for Polite Ladies from Boston." Here Paul has suddenly brought religion down to repentance and to Jesus Christ, "This Way to God." But for the Stoics, lectures about God were much more entertaining.

Luke has pictured Paul like a more modern Socrates, speaking in the agora while accused of promoting foreign divinities. The speech is brilliant, a sharp attack on the idolatries of pop religion that, in many ways, would have appealed to Paul's smart audience. But when Paul turns sermonic, preaching a judgment day, a risen Lord, and an impending future resurrection to judgment, his audience is suddenly turned off.

How can preachers speak on a speech, preach on a preaching? The lection is a tough assignment. We cannot let our sermons turn into an anti-intellectualist attack. Luke himself shows considerable respect for the Greek intellectual tradition. Nor can we simply excoriate the superstitions of popular religion that are prominent in the United States these days. Any sermon, like the speech itself, must get to us; *we* must realize our impending judgment and our need for repentance. Perhaps a sermon can work on the sudden shift from talking about God the creator to talking about the living God of our lives. Even better, maybe our sermons can do the same thing!

SECOND LESSON: 1 PETER 3:13-22

In some lectionaries, the passage is limited to vv. 15-18. A shorter passage has some advantages: vv. 13-14 are somewhat redundant (see 2:18-20) and vv. 19-22 are very obscure. Nevertheless we will review the entire passage.

Does the passage relate to persecution that Christians may have to undergo for the sake of their faith? Probably. But in the first three chapters of 1 Peter, in what appears to be a sermon for the newly baptized, persecution is an off-chance, somewhat romantic, prospect: "Now who will harm you if you are eager to do what is good?" asks the author. He has just quoted from Ps. 34:12, "The eyes of the Lord are on the righteous, and [God's] ears are open to their prayer." First Peter seems to be thinking that, in the unlikely event that Christians are actually persecuted, God will take care of them. What is more, he hints at some gain in suffering. "Even if you do suffer for doing what is right, you are blessed," he says, reversing the beatitude in Matt. 5:10. In the last chapter and a half of his letter, when persecution has actually begun, his message is much less glib. Yet, if somewhat facile, 1 Peter's message is ultimately true. God may not prevent our being persecuted; if we take a strong stand in the name of Christ, we may suffer. Christians in Central America and Africa have been killed in recent years because of their Christian witness. But that God is in a profound way with those martyred is surely true; that God's will is ultimately achieved through martyrdom is as true. Did not the death of Martin Luther King, Jr., further the cause of civil rights in America?

First Peter addresses his congregation, handing out some helpful guidance. He quotes Isa. 8:12-13: "Do not fear what they fear, and do not be intimidated." Instead, "in your hearts sanctify Christ as Lord." The advice is psychologically insightful. Oppression is usually prompted by fear, and fear on the part of the oppressor is strangely contagious. But Christians, whose Lord was beaten up and crucified, can stand in the strength of Christ courageously, neither intimidated nor caught up in violence.

Then there comes a slight shift in focus. The author now offers advice on how to handle accusations: "Always be ready to make your defense to anyone who demands from you an accounting for the hope that is in you" (v. 15b). Here the word for "defense" is a legal term for the testimony of an accused person before the court. We ought to be able to explain reasons for our Christian faith when questioned; something more than, "Jesus loves me this I know/for the Bible tells me so." Yet we must speak our defense with gentleness and respect—no uppity Christians, please. "Keep your conscience clear," 1 Peter advises, so that those who malign you will be "put to shame." Here the idea is that modest, well-behaved Christians will make any charges against them appear contrived; thus accusers will themselves be accused. First Peter's advice is remarkably similar to the training given to participants in the civil rights protests of the 1960s. Early Christianity swept the world when it matched persecution with nonviolent love. ✓

Once more, 1 Peter draws analogy to the sufferings of Christ. "For Christ also suffered for sins once for all, the righteous for the unrighteous, in order to bring you to God" (v. 18). Obviously 1 Peter is putting forth a notion of vicarious suffering. Although the unrighteous deserve punishment, a righteous Christ suffers in their stead (read *our* stead). Therefore he can lead us into the presence of God. The phrase "He was put to death in the flesh, but made alive in the spirit," along with all of v. 18, sounds very much like a liturgical text, which 1 Peter may be quoting. The use of "flesh" and "spirit" in the line may imply agency: Christ was murdered by human powers (flesh) but now is alive by the power of God (spirit). The text is definitely not saying that Christ's flesh died but his spirit is alive.

The odd reference in v. 19 about Christ preaching to "the spirits in prison" has puzzled scholars for centuries. What on earth does the phrase mean? Is it a reference to the unrepentant dead who were swept away in Noah's flood? Is Christ giving them a chance to be saved? Some Byzantine icons picture Christ as a warrior wielding his cross to shatter the prison doors of Hades so that the dead may walk free in mercy. Or maybe the reference is to fallen angels who once coupled with the good-looking daughters of humanity in Gen. 6:1-2 and who, in part, occasioned the flood. Some interpreters have put the odd reference together with the creed: "He descended into hell," but there is no reference here in 1 Peter to a descent.

Mention of the flood and Noah's deliverance prompts a somewhat clumsy analogy with baptism. First Peter observes that the ritual of baptism does not wash away sins like "dirt from the body." Rather in baptism we stand before God in "good conscience, through the resurrection of Jesus Christ." Early Christians did connect baptism with the story of Noah's flood. In baptism we pass through the flood and stand free in the rainbow promise of God. Likewise Christians believed that the risen Christ had passed through the judgment and been acquitted; we, therefore, joined to Christ by faith, are also acquitted.

Then 1 Peter pictures Christ raised to the "right hand of God," where "angels, authorities, and powers" are now subject to him. Why does 1 Peter mention authorities and powers? Perhaps because he believes they are responsible for stirring up persecution. But if Christ is now enthroned beside God, we Christians need not fear persecution. Ultimately we are secure in the power of the risen Christ.

No doubt the lectionaries that reduce the scope of the passage are wise. Verses 15b-18 alone will shape a fine sermon. The problem: Most American Christians are not hauled into court for their convictions. They seldom, if ever, have to give an account of their faith. Has our Christian faith been so tamed by society that it no longer troubles the world around us? Yet if we live Christian faith truly, we will collide with cultural values—racism, militarism, capitalism, and so forth. Maybe the passage calls us to radical Christianity as well as forthright courage.

42

GOSPEL: JOHN 14:15-21

Many scholars have noticed a kind of triadic design to John 14:15-24. Verses 15-17 are concerned with the gift of the Spirit-Paraclete; vv. 18-21 with a coming again of Jesus, and vv. 22-24 with the presence of the "Father." Each of the three sections underscores a connection between obedience and love (vv. 17, 21, 23). For unknown reasons, most lectionaries feature only the first two parts of the triad.

A peculiarity of the Gospel of John is its use of the term *Paraclete* (Gk. *parakletos*), which the NRSV translates "Advocate." In a footnote, the NRSV adds another possible translation, "Helper." The word is notoriously difficult to define. Yes, the Paraclete is an advocate, interceding before God on behalf of the disciples. Likewise the Paraclete is a helper, strengthening Christian faith and faithfulness particularly in times of trial. But the Paraclete is also "the Spirit of truth" (v. 17). As a result, the Paraclete brings to mind Jesus and interprets the truth of his words; thus the Paraclete is an interpreter who informs brave Christian proclamation. Indeed, it is through *interpretation* that the Paraclete helps us—comforting, strengthening, and holding firm. Moreover, as the Spirit of truth, the Paraclete exposes the falsity of the world. Thus, though the Gospel of John promises the Holy Spirit, his emphases are unique. Like the sectarian Essenes of the Qumran community, he speaks of a "Spirit of truth," namely, the Paraclete.

The passage begins with a somewhat enigmatic statement: "If you love me, you will keep my commandments." The statement is startling to us because these days love is largely a feeling, a spontaneous, warm, fuzzy feeling. How can a feeling be commanded? And how can spontaneity be ethically obedient? We forget that in the Bible more often than not, love is action not a feeling; it is something you do. Therefore, if we love Christ, then presumably we will do his will. Although v. 15 talks of keeping commandments, our obedience will scarcely be slavish; in love, obedience will be a free, eager, voluntary willingness.

Then in v. 16 Jesus promises "another Advocate [Paraclete], to be with you forever." The word *another* is a tip-off. Apparently Jesus regards himself as a Paraclete—interceding, helping, and interpreting the truth of God. So here he promises to ask that "another Paraclete" be given to the disciples. The world will be unable to know the unseen presence of the Spirit/Paraclete, just as the world is incapable of recognizing Jesus. But disciples will know because the Spirit "abides with you and

. . . will be among you." So Jesus promises the Spirit for the community of faith.

Then, somewhat abruptly, a change of focus occurs in v. 18: "I will not leave you orphaned; I am coming to you," says Jesus. The metaphor, "orphaned," was a familiar image used of disciples after the death of a well-loved rabbi or with reference to the students of Socrates. On a more profound level, all human beings at some time or another feel a kind of orphaned aloneness in a world that can seem large and alien. Antoine de St.-Exupéry, a pilot, recalled crash-landing in the Sahara. He lay flat on his back on sand beneath the wide wheel of night stars and, according to his diary, felt absolutely orphaned. But Jesus announces, "I am coming to you." No doubt his words refer to Easter Day resurrection appearances, when, according to John 20:20, "the disciples rejoiced when they saw the Lord." But the verse must also relate to the ambiguity of 14:3, "I will come again and take you to myself," which seemingly hints at the hope of glory. Does the phrase "on that day" (v. 20) intend not only Easter but the day when God's ultimate purposes will be fulfilled? "Because I live, you also will live. On that day, you will know that I am in my Father, and you in me, and I in you." The Gospel of John seems to look for some final geometry of love in glory.

In v. 21 the passage seems to circle back on itself: "They who have my commandments and keep them are those who love me." Many preachers tend to reduce the Gospel of John to a kind of misty relational feeling of faith/love/peace/joy. But being one with Jesus involves action, not merely a hot-tub experience of mystical togetherness. Union with Christ is defined by ethical rigor. How is Christ in us ultimately? Christ is in us as we do works of love, his agapic love, which is, of course, God's love.

The Ascension of Our Lord

Lutheran	Roman Catholic	Episcopal	Common Lectionary
Acts 1:1-11	Acts 1:1-11	Acts 1:1-11	Acts 1:1-11
Eph. 1:16-23	Eph. 1:17-23	Eph. 1:15-23	Eph. 1:15-23
Luke 24:44-53	Matt. 28:16-20	Luke 24:49-53	Luke 24:46-53 or Mark 16:9-16, 19-20

FIRST LESSON: ACTS 1:1-11

In an eastern city, there is a Church of the Ascension that features a painting of Jesus floating up on a cloud in the sky. A little girl visited the church with her father. "Why is Jesus up in the air," she asked. A good question. Luke tells the story of Jesus' ascension twice, at the end of his Gospel and again at the beginning of Acts. To modern minds the story is quite incredible—startled disciples, white-robed angels, and Jesus riding a rising cloud. Yet, though Ascension Day may not be celebrated in all churches, it is theologically crucial.

Many scholars suppose that resurrection, ascension, and the gift of the Spirit were once all associated with the great event of Easter. But Luke seems to have stretched them into three different moments in the history of the early church—Easter, Ascension, and, finally, Pentecost. As a result, our church year retains three separate celebrations.

Why is Jesus up in the air? Why is Ascension Day a crucial *theological festival*? (1) Ascension Day is politically important. It celebrates the Lordship of Christ. If Jesus Christ is enthroned "at the right hand of God," then our primary obedience is to him, and all earthly authorities—kings, presidents, dictators—are demoted. We need not cling to mythological language—talk of thrones and rising bright clouds—in order to affirm ultimate loyalty to Christ. Political courage on the part of Christians, such as conscientious objection and refusal to pay full taxes, begins with a notion of Christ's Lordship. (2) Ascension Day assists a true Christian devotion. We remember that Christ is risen, and, in spite of cloying Jesus piety, he is not here. No wonder that early Christian worship would cry with eager longing, "Maranatha— Lord come!" Can we have a true understanding of the Holy Spirit without honestly admitting the absence of Christ? (3) Ascension Day

45

is a theological celebration, for we affirm that the crucified one has been taken up into the godhead. Now we cannot possibly conceive of God apart from recalling the crucified and risen Lord Christ. Churches ought to recover Ascension Day; theologically it is central to Christian conviction.

The passage in Acts 1:1-11 is complicated, however. The lection begins with a kind of "proem." Ancient writers when beginning a second volume in series would often repeat a dedication from their first volume by naming a name ("Theophilus"), often the name of a sponsor. They would also refer back to the first volume, "In the first book . . . ," and usually summarize its contents: "I wrote about all that Jesus did and taught." In vv. 2-3 Luke recalls his story from beginning to end. Although most proems then turn to summarize the action to be forthcoming in a new volume, Luke does not. Instead he rehearses the resurrection appearances and retells the story of the ascension.

In v. 2 Luke reinforces apostolic authority; the apostles were chosen under the guidance of the Holy Spirit, and they were tutored carefully in the faith by the risen Christ. Then in v. 3 Luke changes his own story. In the last chapter of his Gospel, resurrection and ascension seem to happen on the same day. But now Luke speaks of forty days between resurrection on Easter Day and the Ascension. Forty days match the forty years in the wilderness and the forty days between Christ's baptism and the inauguration of his ministry (Luke 4:2).

Then Acts recalls a specific incident when the disciples were gathered at table with the risen Lord (the word *staying* in the NRSV can mean eating). Christ had told them to wait for "what my Father promised" (Luke 24:49). Then Luke speaks a saying originally from the lips of John the Baptist (Luke 3:16): "John baptized with water, but you will be baptized with the Holy Spirit." The new age of the Spirit with the church will soon begin.

In the next two verses, Luke quashes all speculation about the parousia, when and where. The disciples ask when Christ will usher in the kingdom. Jesus firmly answers: "It is not for you to know the times or periods that the Father has set by his own authority." By the time of Luke's writing, the sense of an immediate end to "this present age" and of a looming apocalyptic "new aeon" had clearly ebbed. In Luke's mind, now is time for a Christian mission: "You will receive power when the Holy Spirit has come upon you; and you will be my witnesses in Jerusalem, in all Judea and Samaria, and to the ends of the earth"

(v. 8). The young church is here commissioned and missionary journeys prefigured.

The actual ascension is definitely a problem. At the end of his Gospel, Luke recounts an ascension, and now, forty days later, do we have another? Some scholars believe that Luke 24 did not originally end with the ascension and in fact have some manuscript evidence to support their contention. Others argue that Luke-Acts was originally one volume and that some subsequent editor penned a repetitive introduction. Most likely, Luke is clarifying his own earlier work with the symbolic addition of the forty days. The actual description of the ascension is modest compared with the hoopla in some legendary accounts, such as the apocryphal *Gospel of Peter*. In Acts 1:10-11 two angels show up, like the angels at the tomb, to explain the event. Christians need not stand staring into the heavens, looking for the Lord. The Lord will return. Meanwhile we wait for the Spirit so as to inaugurate our proper evangelical mission in the world.

Angels and a cloud-riding Christ make the story of the ascension difficult for us modern, overliteral readers of Scripture. But Ascension Day is theologically profound, and, although we may have to be honest about fairy-tale images, we can go for the theological wonders of the story.

SECOND LESSON: EPHESIANS 1:15-23

In the Greek, the passage comprises one long clausal sentence. First-century letters conventionally contained both "I give thanks . . ." and "I pray that . . ." sections. Some letters also featured "Blessed be . . ." sections. Ephesians contains all of these forms. There is a blessing section, vv. 3-14, followed by the more usual "thanksgiving" and "intercession" formulas in vv. 15-23. But, though the forms are familiar, in Ephesians they are crammed with meaning.

Scholars have analyzed the thanksgiving and intercession formulas in the letters of the Christian Scriptures. They are found in all the letters except Galatians. The letters always include a thanksgiving and usually the mention of "hearing" reports. In Ephesians the writer is thankful because he has heard reports of the congregation's fidelity and their charity toward "the saints" (v. 15). A reference to prayer follows immediately: "I remember you in my prayers" (v. 16). The writer heaps up intercessions. May the Ephesians have "a spirit of wisdom and revelation" to know God profoundly, that is, "with the eyes of your heart" (vv. 17-18). May they also know the "hope to which [God] has called you," the "glorious inheritance," as well as the miraculous power of God in their common lives.

Then the writer seems to be quoting from a hymn, or some sort of liturgical material, in vv. 20b-22 (23?). We might read these verses in the following way:

> [20] [God] raised him from among the dead
>   and set him at the right hand in heavenly places
> [21] above every rule and authority and power and dominion
>   and every name named, not only in this age but the coming one.
> [22] [God] put under his feet all things
>   and gave him to be head over all things.

Is v. 23 part of the hymn? Scholars are divided. We shall assume that the author of Ephesians, who is probably not the apostle Paul, is adding to the hymn a reference to the church as Christ's body. The final phrase "the fullness of him who fills all in all" may have been drawn from the hymn or may be a kind of coda that the writer himself designed.

The passage is not easy to interpret. There are references to "principalities and powers," to "the body of Christ," to "fullness"—all difficult ideas to grasp, much less preach. Let us discuss them in order.

Who are the "principalities and powers"? Apparently they are heavenly forces, perhaps angelic beings, who sway political, social, and religious affairs on earth. Apparently they could take over and control human values, beliefs, and what we term life-styles. Nowadays we may think of transsocial attitudes, ideals, ideas, and images that seem to influence human patterns of thought—everything from patriotism to NFL values ("Winning isn't everything, it's the only thing") to changing fashions to TV religion. The "powers that be" can so easily take us captive. Although seldom noticed, they get at us through crowd culture, advertising, media. The writer of Ephesians sees the principalities and powers as invisible enemies with which Christians must do battle (Eph. 6:10-20). He looks forward to a day when Christ will bring the powers under control, so they may bow before the throne of God.

What of "the head of the body"? The word *head* is used much as we do today when we refer to the head of a corporation or to heads of state. And, as in our usage, *head* can also mean a controlling part of the body. In Greek Stoic thought, we find notions of the universe as God's body—thus God is the *head* of all things. From the head of the body comes all wisdom, motive, reason, power, command, and so on. Thus Paul is not using *body* as an identity word—that is, the church = Christ—but rather relationally; Christ is head of the body of the church, giving her life, purpose, and understanding. Many preachers seem now to be using the phrase "body of Christ" triumphantly to give the church status. But on earth the church is bodily (and may well become a broken body), and it takes orders from its head, the risen, regal Christ. In Ephesians, Christ is said to be "head over all things," perhaps a quote from Ps. 8:6. So Christ enthroned is regarded as a messianic ruler of the whole world as well as head of the church.

The word *fullness* is more complex. It seems to go along with the notion of "all things," which frequently means "universe." God's "fullness" would be the total of divine attributes—God's wisdom, truth, life, glory, and so forth. Thus the term can convey both amplitude, an overflowingness, and a complete perfection. In the Gospel of John (1:16), we are told that from Christ's "fullness we have all received, grace upon grace." Here in Ephesians (v. 23), the fullness of God in Christ fills the church, all in all.

So Ephesians sings a hymn that might have been written for Ascension Day. God has raised up Jesus Christ to be the head over all things. Ephesians lists "all things": every rule, authority, power, dominion, and every name named, now and forever! "All things"—Ephesians uses the phrase twice and, in case we missed the meaning, concludes with "all in all." Resurrection does not merely celebrate an open grave, that is, rescue from death. Resurrection affirms the raising of Christ to a position of authority. Who ultimately rules the world? The God revealed in Christ our Lord.

But then spot the wild surmise: The author of Ephesians is convinced that the power of God, the same power that raised up Christ, is at work in and through the church. By the power of the resurrection, then, there is faithfulness and charity in Ephesus. And just as Christ has been raised, so our hope is similar. The idea of the fullness of God's power being at work among us two-legged, plain-faced, bumbling, bored, off-key-singing, reluctant Christians is astonishing. The fullness of God filled Jesus Christ and in turn fills the church with "the spirit of wisdom and revelation." Tucked away in a difficult passage is an amazing gospel message.

GOSPEL: LUKE 24:44-53

The Gospel of Matthew (28:16-20) concludes with Christ perched on top of a mountain handing out what usually is called the Great Commission to his awed disciples—"Go into all the world . . ." Here is Luke's version of a final commissioning, and in a way it is even more spectacular, for it concludes with Christ hoisted skyward into the heavens.

The passage begins with an obscurity: "These are my words that I spoke to you while I was still with you." What words did he speak, where and when? Is he referring back to his sermon on the Emmaus road, vv. 25-27, or to some earlier teachings recorded in Luke's Gospel? He continues: "everything written about me in the law of Moses, the prophets, and the psalms must be fulfilled." The idea that Christ's life, death, and resurrection fulfill scriptural prophecy is a favorite Lukan theme. Notice how sweeping his sources are; he cites not only the Torah ("the law of Moses") but prophets and the Psalms as well. For Luke, all Scripture testifies to Jesus Christ.

But then "he opened their minds to understand the scriptures." Christ hands out an interpretive clue. "Thus it is written," he says, "that the Messiah is to suffer and to rise from the dead on the third day." We can speculate as to what passages of Scripture Luke has in mind. Is he thinking of servant passages in second Isaiah, Isaiah 53 for example, or of Psalms such as 22 and 69, which refer to suffering? Or does he recall Hos. 6:2, "After two days he will revive us; on the third day he will raise us up, that we may live before him"? We have no way of knowing. But the fulfillment of Scripture is important to Luke because it certifies that Christ's passion and resurrection are part of God's planned purpose from the beginning of time.

Now comes the commissioning: "repentance and forgiveness of sins is to be proclaimed in his name to all nations, beginning from Jerusalem." The disciples are also part of God's plan. They are chosen "witnesses of these things." Their ministry is a fulfillment of prophecy: "For out of Zion shall go forth instruction, and the word of the Lord from Jerusalem" (Isa. 2:3; Mic. 4:2). But notice that their message is "repentance and forgiveness," which will be the way in which all the missionary speeches in Acts will conclude—the Christ whom we crucified, God has raised up; therefore repent and accept God's mercy.

Although the disciples are commissioned, they must wait for the coming of the Holy Spirit. Why does Jesus refer to the promised Holy

Spirit as being "*clothed* with power from on high"? Perhaps Luke is alluding to the story of Elijah clothing Elisha before being taken up into the heavens (2 Kings 2:1-14).

Then Jesus leads the twelve disciples out to Bethany, where he began his entry into Jerusalem, and there he blesses them. The Bible has many last blessing stories: blessings by Jacob (Gen. 48:20), by Moses (Deut. 33:1), by King Solomon (1 Kings 8:54f), and in the apocryphal book Tobit, a blessing by the angel Raphael before an ascension. But Christ's blessing completes a gesture left undone by a mute Zechariah at the beginning of the Gospel (1:21-22) and thus provides closure for Luke's volume.

Verse 51 is uncertain: In some manuscripts the phrase "and was carried up into heaven" is missing, as is the following "and they worshiped him." Nevertheless most manuscripts feature an ascension, perhaps modeled on the Elijah-Elisha story. Christ is lifted to the "right hand of God," where he will command the life of the church. No wonder the disciples return to the city and, awaiting the Spirit, "were continually in the temple blessing God."

The passage speaks to us today. We are commissioned people. Our head is the risen Christ, and our energy is his compelling Spirit. But we are not merely an afterthought created by the departing Lord; we are part of God's long-term saving purpose. From the beginning God brought us Jesus Christ, gave him the Spirit, drew him to Jerusalem to die and rise and be enthroned. From the beginning God ordained a discipleship and promised them the same Spirit that was in Christ Jesus. They would go out from Jerusalem preaching mercy to the whole wide world. Though Christ is not here, we are. We speak the word of the risen Lord, we share his Spirit, and we do his work in the world. The word of mercy is now on our lips.

Seventh Sunday of Easter

Lutheran	Roman Catholic	Episcopal	Common Lectionary
Acts 1:8-14	Acts 1:12-14	Acts 1:8-14	Acts 1:6-14
1 Pet. 4:12-17, 5:6-11	1 Pet. 4:13-16	1 Pet. 4:12-19	1 Pet. 4:12-14, 5:6-11
John 17:1-11	John 17:1-11a	John 17:1-11	John 17:1-11

FIRST LESSON: ACTS 1:8-14

The reading for the Sunday after Ascension Day picks up some of the story of the ascension (vv. 8-11) plus a summary depiction of the early Christian community (vv. 12-14).

In retelling the ascension, the lection begins with v. 8. The disciples were chosen by Christ (Luke 6:12-16), commissioned with the gospel message (Luke 9:1-6), and now are to be witnesses. They will tell what they have seen and heard, namely, the words of Christ, his death and resurrection, which fulfill the Scriptures, as well as his mercy and a call to repentance. Jesus chose disciples, but the resurrection and ascension created apostolic witnesses. Notice that the description "in Jerusalem, in all Judea and Samaria, and to the ends of the earth" seems to spiral out from Jerusalem in a widening circle, matching the story Luke will tell in Acts.

Why is the apostolic ministry necessary? Because risen, Christ is not here. All the resurrection texts underscore Christ's exaltation; he is not here precisely because he is enthroned as a messianic regent at the right hand of God. Luke dares to picture his enthronement. Like Elijah (2 Kings 2:11), Jesus is lifted up into heaven on a cloud, and now, like Elisha, the church will soon receive the mantle of his Spirit. Two angels, similar to the angels at the tomb (Luke 24:4-7), appear and clue in the awed disciples: "Men of Galilee, why do you stand looking up toward heaven?" (Why are angels so pedantic?) They then inform the disciples that Christ will return the same way he has departed, presumably on a cloud. Luke thus defers the second coming. Meanwhile we need not gaze up like the two tramps in *Waiting for Godot*. Instead we can be about the work of the Lord. Notice that two themes connected with Ascension Day are enunciated here: the departure of Christ (he is not here) and his enthronement (he is the Lord).

The ascension corrects all our mawkish Jesus piety. Jesus is not the unseen guest, he is not a sweet inner spookiness in our hearts, he does not wander our gardens when the dew is still on the roses. If risen, then he is not here. At the same time, the ascension is political dynamite. If Christ is enthroned as the Lord of the world, then neither our nations nor our own political leaders have ultimate status. Why does the book of Acts picture early Christians as surprisingly brave and even slightly impudent in the presence of political power? Because Christ alone is Lord, and everyone else in power is wrapped in the emperor's new clothes; that is, stripped of the aura of office, they are no more than human beings. So, "as they were watching, he was lifted up."

In Acts the apostles must wait for ten days from the time of the ascension until finally, empowered by the Holy Spirit, their ministry can begin. Therefore they return to Jerusalem from the Mount of Olives, "a sabbath day's journey." A sabbath day's journey was the 960 yards that were allowed pious Jews on the sabbath without breaching the law (Exod. 16:29). Was the Mount of Olives mentioned because of a traditional belief that the Messiah would descend there (Zech. 14:4), or because Jesus led his disciples there for prayer (Luke 22:39-46)? The disciples return to the city and devote themselves to prayer. Acts pictures them gathered in an "upper room," perhaps fulfilling the words of Dan. 6:10.

The names of the disciples are listed in a slightly different order than in Luke 6:12-16. Peter and John are at the head of the list, and James, who according to 1 Cor. 15:7 was a witness to the resurrection, follows. There are eleven names in all, one short of the symbolic twelve. Verse 14 adds to the disciples "certain women" who were also engaged in prayerful waiting. Presumably these are women mentioned in Luke's Gospel as supporters of Jesus (8:2; 23:49, 55; 24:10). They have been faithful (while the disciples fled) and were also witnesses to the resurrection. More, they are in continuity with the women who subsequently will be mentioned in Acts as supporters or leaders of the Christian community. The reference to Mary, Jesus' mother, and to "his brothers" is somewhat surprising inasmuch as they considered him "beside himself" as well as something of a family disgrace (Luke 3:31-35). But they are included and no doubt did receive special respect in the early church.

The message of the ascension is important: Christ is enthroned and we are his chosen witnesses, both women and men. Although Christ is gone from sight, we continue his ministry, preaching and teaching and healing and praying—much too busy for heaven gazing.

SECOND LESSON: 1 PETER 4:12-19; 5:6-11

Some scholars suppose that the bulk of 1 Peter is a baptismal sermon that ends with a doxology and a final Amen in verse 4:11. Then, past eloquence over, in verse 4:12 cruel reality intrudes. Once upon a time baptismal candidates were exhorted to suffer persecution with courage, should persecution befall them. Now they are persecuted; the old sermon has come true: "Beloved do not be surprised at the fiery ordeal that is taking place."

The original sermon was remarkably prescient. Had 1 Peter not spoken of righteous suffering? Had he not urged the newly baptized to suffer with Christ patiently? In the midst of a "fiery ordeal!" (were martyrs actually being burned?) the preacher tells his Christian comrades to be true to their baptism in Christ.

Verse 13 should not be read as a promise of reward; that is, suffer with Christ now, and later you will be paid off in glory. Right now Christians may rejoice in the "fellowship" of suffering with Christ. If they are one with Christ now, they will be one with Christ in glory as well. The exhortation is followed up in v. 14 with an allusion to one of the Beatitudes: "Blessed are you when people revile you and persecute you and utter all kinds of evil against you falsely on my account" (Matt. 5:11).

In v. 16 the term *Christian* appears. The word is found only two other times in the New Testament (Acts 11:26; 26:28). *Christian* probably was a term of derision used by persecutors, much as the word *Christer* is used today. But, possibly because of brave martyrs, *Christian* became a proud title. The author of 1 Peter thus urges his audience to glorify God for the name Christian; after all they are not suffering as murderers, thieves, or criminals, but as Christians.

Then 1 Peter speaks of judgment: With terrible persecutions, God's judgment has begun "with the household of God." God's judgment will end with an even more fearful punishment of those who "do not obey the gospel of God." First Peter supports this rather ungenerous observation with a quote from Prov. 11:31. Even a hint of hand-rubbing glee over the torments of others, however, is unbecoming, despite 1 Peter and a few other Christian writers.

The lectionary has added exhortations from 5:6-11. The material is addressed to church leadership, "As an elder myself, . . . I exhort the elders among you" (5:1), although later it is extended to "all of you" (5:5). In this section, 1 Peter urges humility. Then after quoting a version of Ps. 55:22 in v. 7, he charges his listeners to resist the devil, who "prowls around, looking for someone to devour" (v. 8). He calls the devil "your adversary." Contemporary preachers need not reinstate a literal notion of the devil in order to proclaim the passage; human evil is quite apparent to us all without having recourse to the devil. Although the notion of a devil is biblical (see Job 1:6-12), it was enlarged by the mythology of Persian dualism. Evil is evil, but no matter how organized or cosmic in character, it still is stamped with a human trademark.

What does 1 Peter offer to encourage those who must face persecution? (1) The joy of union with the Christ who suffered (4:13); (2) the knowledge that you share suffering with sisters and brothers in Christ (v. 9); and (3) the hope that suffering will be brief. Then God, who has called us to eternal glory in Christ, will help us. First Peter heaps up four verbs: restore, support, strengthen, and establish (vv. 10-11).

All human pain can be a sharing of the suffering of Christ, but 1 Peter is specifically written to Christians who are being persecuted. In North America nobody seems to be hurting us, at least not because we are Christians. Perhaps then the passage must be turned to address the reality of human pain per se. A hangnail may not quite qualify us for union with Christ, but sooner or later most human beings will suffer. Suffering is seldom automatically ennobling, and indeed can grind us down; yet in faith, suffering can join us tenderly to fellow human beings and devoutly to the crucified Christ. A Puerto Rican friend of mine, a house painter, tumbled from a high ladder onto concrete. He shrieked in pain, "Why, why, why, why, why?!" Suddenly he interrupted himself and said, "Jesus hurt," and thereafter bore his pain with astonishing patience.

GOSPEL: JOHN 17:1-11

Chapter 17 of the Gospel of John has traditionally been labeled Jesus' "high priestly prayer." Pagan literature contains many farewell discourses, that is, representations of last speeches by famous people. Final prayers also exist in pagan literature, as well as in biblical books (see Deuteronomy 32). But, though designed with unusual care as a model prayer, John 17 appears to be quite different. Scholars tend to divide the prayer into sections, some of which are demarked by the address "Father": Verses 1-5 pray for Jesus' glorification; vv. 6-11a refer to the disciples; vv. 11b-19 pray for the protection and sanctification of the disciples; vv. 20-24 pray for future believers; and vv. 25-26 conclude the prayer with a reiteration of the theme of unity. The lection includes only the first two parts of the prayer.

Underlying the discourses and the prayer is a high Johannine Christology. For in the Gospel of John, Jesus sets aside his glory as God's Son, descends to the human world in Jesus of Nazareth, and, when his work is complete, ascends to the "Father" again through being lifted up on the cross and then raised from the tomb. Thus Christ comes from glory and returns to glory. Johannine Christology is somewhat like the pattern of thought to be found in the famous Christ hymn of Philippians 2: Christ divested himself of glory, took the form of a servant, was obedient to the point of death, and "therefore God also highly exalted him" (Phil. 2:9).

The prayer begins solemnly: "Father, the hour has come." The hour is the time of Christ's being "lifted up," not only on the cross but, through resurrection, to God. The phrase "glorify your Son so that the Son may glorify you" seems to echo 13:31-32, with which the farewell discourses began. Verses 4-5 elaborate the same themes. Jesus says that he has glorified God by doing the work he was given to do on earth, namely, bringing eternal life to those whom God elected (v. 2). Therefore, his work all but completed, he prays, "Father, glorify me . . . with the glory that I had in your presence before the world existed." Remember that in John, Jesus is the divine Son of God who descends from glory and will return to glory once more.

Verse 3 is much quoted: "This is eternal life, that they may know you, the only true God, and Jesus Christ whom you have sent." Many scholars suspect that the verse is an editorial addition to the prayer; and it probably is, for nowhere else does Jesus refer to himself by name and title, Jesus Christ. Other scholars have called the verse an example of Johannine Gnosticism because it seems to define salvation as knowing (*gnosis*). But in the Gospel of John, knowing is never an acquired esoteric knowledge; knowing is by doing or by communion. Thus to know God is to be in communion with God and to do God's perfect will.

With v. 6 the prayer shifts in focus. Jesus refers to his disciples: "I have made your name known to those whom you gave me from the world." When John speaks of making God's name known, he uses *name* in a biblical way to mean God's divine nature. Again and again, Jesus has spoken the divine name, "I am," and then, through metaphors, spoken of the God he reveals as "bread of life," "good shepherd," "true vine," "light of the world," and so forth. Jesus seems to be saying that the disciples, whom God has elected, have been schooled in the truth of God (vv. 7-8). Finally, in v. 11 he announces, I am coming to you, "but they are in the world." Then he prays with great intensity, "Holy Father, protect them . . . so that they may be one."

In John the discipleship continues the work of Jesus Christ. Although Christ has ascended to the "Father," the disciples will take his place. They are one with Christ in purpose and are therefore one with God. Christ prays for their undivided unity. The prayer "that they may be one" is a judgment on our divided and subdivided denominationalism. Division in the church, whether it be denominational or political— conservatives, liberals, moderates—is always a violation of Christ's own deep holy purpose for us and, therefore, a wickedness. How can we be one with Christ and the "Father" if we ourselves are divided?

In a short story there is a scene in which a young boy overhears his father praying, and not only praying, but praying for him. All through life, and even after his father was gone, he remembered the moment when he overheard his father praying for him. Here in the Gospel of John, we are allowed to overhear Jesus Christ praying for us. We can be surprised by his confidence in us: "they have kept your word," "they know in truth," "they have believed." We are moved by his concern: "Holy Father, protect them." In our discipleship we must never forget that we have been prayed for by Jesus Christ, Son of God, who is from glory and now, once more, has been glorified.

The Day of Pentecost

Lutheran	Roman Catholic	Episcopal	Common Lectionary
Joel 2:28-29	Acts 2:1-11	Acts 2:1-11	Acts 2:1-21 or Isa. 44:1-8
Acts 2:1-21	1 Cor. 12:3b-7, 12-13	1 Cor. 12:4-13	1 Cor. 12:3b-13 or Acts 2:1-21
John 20:19-23	John 20:19-23	John 20:19-23	John 20:19-23 or John 7:37-39

FIRST LESSON: ACTS 2:1-11

There are two stories about the giving of the Holy Spirit, one in John 20:19-23 and the other in Acts 2. In John's account, resurrection, ascension, and the gift of the Spirit are joined; they all occur on Easter Day. Many scholars suppose that John's account reflects a more primitive tradition. Luke tells quite a different story. In Acts the Holy Spirit is poured out on Pentecost, fifty days after Easter. Although Pentecost was originally an agricultural festival (Lev. 23:15f.), Jewish rabbis celebrated the giving of the law on Pentecost. Did early Christians create a competitive festival for the giving of the Spirit?

How much actual history underlies Acts 2:1-11? We cannot say. As it stands, the story is highly symbolic with its eerie wind and spectacular split-up flames. A Jewish legend tells of how the voice of God was divided into seventy languages at Sinai. In Acts 2 the word of God, empowered by the Spirit, is heard in many languages, perhaps as a sign of the forthcoming Christian mission. The story of Pentecost, as many preachers have noticed, reverses the babble of Babel and promises a profound unity to the world.

The story begins solemnly: "When the day of Pentecost had come." In Greek the words clearly recall Luke 9:51, "When the days drew near for him to be taken up . . . ," which commences the story of the passion. In each case, predictions came (9:22, 31, 44, and for Pentecost, Luke 24:49 and Acts 1:4-5, 8) before a formal announcement of "the day." But the Pentecost story also recalls the commencement of Christ's ministry. Both accounts contain a conferral of the Spirit (Luke 3:21-22 and Acts 2:2-4) as well as a speech that cites Hebrew Scripture

(Luke 4:18-19 and Acts 2:17-21). In each case the scriptural citation seems to prefigure a mission that follows. Such parallels are scarcely accidental; the church will continue the mission of Jesus Christ, a mission that, like Jesus' own ministry, will be empowered by the Holy Spirit.

Acts 2 tells of the coming of the Spirit dramatically by describing miraculous happenings before any explanation is offered. Suddenly there is a rush of unseen wind followed by forks of flame dividing among all the disciples, a flame for each one. In Greek the word for wind (*pnoa*) and the word for Spirit (*pneuma*) are closely related. As for "tongues, as of fire," although their description may be drawn from Isa. 5:24, they fulfill the prediction of John the Baptist (Luke 3:16) of one who will baptize with "holy Spirit and fire." In v. 4 we are told the meaning of wind and fire, "all of them were filled with the Holy Spirit."

The miraculous speaking "in other languages" has prompted much scholarly debate. Is Acts describing an outbreak of primitive glossolalia? No. Verse 8, "And how is it that we hear, each of us, in our own native language?" makes it quite clear that the disciples, although Galileans, are miraculously enabled to speak in many different languages. The speaking in different tongues is a sign of the future, when the gospel will be preached in many languages all over the world.

No wonder that Acts follows up the miracle with a list of nations. Basically the list moves out from Jerusalem to the wider world, circling from east to west. Scholars suppose that Luke has picked up the list from a much earlier source because Elamites and Medes had already disappeared from history. In addition, scholars also suppose that editorial additions have increased the number of nations mentioned to fourteen; they suspect that Acts originally listed a symbolic twelve. But the conclusion to the list, "in our own languages we hear them speaking about God's deeds of power," demonstrates the evangelical symbolism intended. From Jerusalem the gospel will be preached in every language to every nation—even in English and to us!

How do we preach the Pentecost story? If we adopt a "this is what happened" historical style we could lose the symbolic depth of the account, which is crucial. Maybe we are meant to begin not with the story itself but where we are now, that is, in churches. Our churches are still evangelical; we spread news of "God's deeds of power" in every language. (How many tongues are represented by Bible Society translations?) Still we are on fire with faith.

Where did the gospel come from? We can trace our way back through frontier missionary preachers, to Reformers, to early church leaders such as Francis, Augustine, and Chrysostom, to the twelve apostles, all the way back to the cross. Basically our churches began with Jesus Christ and, after the resurrection, with the mysterious gift of the Spirit. Still our churches are directed by the word of Christ and animated by his shared Spirit. Guess what? The Holy Spirit is among us unseen as wind, fanning flames of faith, giving us impulse to speak. Pentecost is now.

SECOND LESSON: 1 CORINTHIANS 12:4-13

Some lectionaries begin the lesson with 12:3b. But v. 3b is closely related to vv. 2-3a. Evidently Paul is addressing a congregation that has a sizeable group of charismatics who practice glossolalia, speaking in tongues. He therefore sets up a criterion: "no one speaking by the Spirit of God ever says 'Let Jesus be cursed!' and no one can say 'Jesus is Lord!' except by the Holy Spirit." The verse is peculiar; did people caught up in religious ecstasy of some sort actually exclaim, "Jesus is cursed"? Or could the phrase refer to renouncing Christian affiliation under pressure, as for example before a Roman court under threat of death? We may never know. But the second half of Paul's criterion is valid: We could not confess faith in Jesus as Lord apart from the working of the Spirit.

With v. 4 Paul launches a discourse on the so-called charismata, the gifts of the Spirit. Although the Spirit is poured out on the whole church and is therefore among us, over and above exist gifts of the Spirit—charismata. According to Paul, everyone has some gift, and no one possesses all gifts (not even clergy!). Is Paul referring to what we might term natural talents and abilities? Probably not. More likely he believes that the Spirit can provide gifts to those not naturally endowed, according to the need of the church.

The discourse begins with a bold rhetorical flourish. Verses 4-6 are constructed with parallel syntax and a trinitarian progression. "There are varieties of gifts, but the same Spirit; and there are varieties of services, but the same Lord; and there are varieties of activities, but it is the same God who activates all of them in everyone." Notice that

Paul mentions gifts, services or administrative tasks, and energetic activities—all are from the same Spirit/Lord/God who activates them, all in all. Then he sums his rhetoric up in v. 7: "To each is given the manifestation of the Spirit for the common good." The word *manifestation* is important; we see activity, service, or ability in action, and in so doing we are seeing the Spirit at work among us, that is, manifested.

Although some lectionaries skip the recital of gifts in vv. 8-10, others do not. Much of the list is phrased in series of related statements. To one is given words of wisdom and to another words of knowledge (v. 8). Is Paul drawing a distinction between practical, moral wisdom and theological insight? In vv. 9-10a, he parallels gifts of healing and the working of miracles. Some scholars suppose that "healing" refers to illnesses, whereas "miracles" may include exorcisms. "Prophecy" and "discernment of spirits" seem bunched, as are "tongues" and "interpretation of tongues." Although speaking in tongues was apparently prized in the Corinthian congregation, Paul deliberately lists such gifts last of all. Notice that "faith" in v. 9 seems to disturb the parallel constructions. Was the phrase subsequently added to Paul's list? Surely Paul would expect faith of all Christians and not have considered it an added gift. In v. 11 Paul concludes his recital by affirming that the Spirit allots gifts as the Spirit chooses.

Then quite abruptly, in vv. 12-13, Paul introduces the metaphor of the body and body parts. The metaphor was not original with Paul; it was a favorite among Stoic philosophers and others in the ancient world. In pagan literature the metaphor was usually used to encourage unity and discourage jealousy. Though we are many, in Christ we are one body, says Paul, and then adds a somewhat murky statement: "For in the one Spirit we were all baptized into one body—Jews or Greeks, slaves or free—and we were all made to drink of one Spirit" (v. 13). Notice that the parenthetical comparisons—Jews or Greeks, slaves or free—may well be the basis for discrimination in the Christian community. Here, however, they are dismissed because we all have been "baptized into one body" as working parts. What is more, we are all partakers of one Spirit, the Spirit of God that has been poured out on the church. Is there a hidden reference to the Eucharist in "drink of one Spirit"? Probably not, although sharing one cup is surely analogous to living in one Spirit.

Is the passage difficult to preach? Yes. The passage is difficult because of confusion over the doctrine of the Spirit. Many Americans seem to equate the Spirit with feeling and, in particular, with hoopla religious feelings that are antithetical to reason. In addition, Americans seem to suppose that having the Spirit is an individual thing, something that's handed out with conversion. If we preach from 1 Corinthians 12, we must clearly distinguish between the outpouring of the Holy Spirit on the church and the provision of special gifts, charismata, by the Spirit for the church. The Holy Spirit with the church's corporate spirit is primary. The individual gifts are, in a way, secondary.

We have also mentioned that the Spirit's gifts are emphatically gifts; they are not talents or abilities or even inborn proclivities, as if we could pool our skills and help God out a little. We have nothing to offer. Instead, whatever is needed for the church's mission is given by the power of the Spirit. In Paul's thought (as in our true experience) everything is grace.

GOSPEL: JOHN 20:19-23

In the Gospel of John, Easter, Ascension Day, and Pentecost are all jammed into an instant. They happen in four short verses, 20:19-23. The stylized story in John probably reflects a primitive tradition. Later, Luke-Acts stretches the event into three distinct historical moments occurring over a fifty-day period.

The passage is neither history nor narrative. Instead it might be termed a theological drama, for, after v. 19, every verse expresses still another theological understanding of the church. Thus the passage should not be preached as a "This is what happened once upon a time" sermon. Each verse tells us something about the church today—a peaceable community, a commissioned community, a community of the Spirit, a forgiving community, all constituted by the resurrection of Jesus Christ.

The passage begins on "the first day of the week" in a Jerusalem safe house where the frightened disciples are gathered. The phrase "first day of the week" indicates what soon became the "Lord's Day," that is, the early church's customary time for worship. As for the disciples being locked in and scared out of their wits, we ought to be able to understand them; most oldline Protestant denominations are badly frightened these days—self-preservation has become the agenda. In any event, suddenly (presumably passing through the locked doors) the risen Christ appears. To calm the disciples' fears, he says, "Peace." Then he abruptly displays the wounds on his hands and his side, and "the disciples rejoiced when they saw the Lord." Notice that in the biblical tradition the risen Christ still has wounds. Our Lord who rules at the right hand of God is the wounded, crucified Savior.

Jesus speaks a second time, saying, "Peace be with you." This time the "peace" is a conferral, fulfilling an earlier promise: "Peace I leave with you; my peace I give to you" (14:27). Although many preachers portray Christ's peace as an inner, personal harmony, in the Gospel of John peace is given to the community and is expressed interpersonally. The church is to be a small-scale peaceable kingdom in a contentious world; we are called to show the shape of God's shalom. The corporate life that God gives is reconciled and reconciling.

Then Jesus formally commissions the church, saying, "As the Father sent me, so I send you." In the Gospel of John, God loves the world and therefore sends the Son to bring life and truth to humanity (3:16). Unfortunately the world refuses Christ and condemns him to death. In John the church exists to continue the full life-giving ministry of Jesus Christ, if need be including suffering and dying. As the world turned on Christ, so also will the world persecute disciples. In John the commissioning is not merely evangelical—go preach; it is almost incarnational. We are to do Christ's love and truth in the world. Thus our words are much more than words: "If you forgive the sins of any, they are forgiven."

Scholars have struggled to interpret v. 23b: "If you retain the sins of any, they are retained." An old *Life* magazine carried a remarkable picture of the crowd watching the great civil rights march from Selma to Montgomery. For some, mostly black faces, the march was a sign of joyous liberation; people were laughing and dancing and clapping their hands. But for others, mostly stony white faces, it hardened opposition. Surely the gospel functions in much the same way. To the oppressed it is very good news indeed, but to those who have bought into the world's patterns of oppression, it can result in a hardened heart. By their own choice their sin is "retained."

In v. 22 the passage turns spooky. Jesus exhales—whoosh! He breathes into the disciples, saying, "Receive the Holy Spirit." We hear the words and can't help but recall the second chapter of Genesis, where God, having created Earthling [*Ahdam*] out of the earth, "breathed into his nostrils the breath of life; and the man became a living being" (Gen. 2:7). Here Jesus breathes the breath of new life—

second-Adam, new-creation life—into the gathered community. They receive the Spirit so as to fulfill their commissioned, life-giving ministry.

A few years ago there was a British film about a man from Calcutta, India, who came to London to find fame and fortune. During his first week in the city, he saw a woman struck by a bus. She lay in the street, not breathing. So the little man rushed over, applied mouth-to-mouth resuscitation, and revived her. He stood and announced proudly, "Madam, my life is in you now!" Perhaps John is trying to express the same idea by having Christ breathe the Spirit into the gathered disciples: "My life is in you now!"

We have said that John 20:19-23 is neither history nor story. There is no real moving plot in the words. Instead the passage is contrived theologically. John is portraying the true meaning of church. The church is re-created by the resurrection of Jesus Christ; it is commissioned, granted peace, told a message of mercy, and given the Holy Spirit, the same Spirit that was in Christ Jesus. Why is the church in the world? Because God loves the world. God's special child Jesus Christ has in turn created disciples to carry on his calling. Who are the disciples? Us, that's who.